CW00544427

Sent From Nicky!

Best wishes,

David M

A FEW MORE LAPS

Foreword

I thought I had known David forever but like all good books this puts me straight; he is 14 years younger than me. We do have many things in common though, as I remember most, though not all, of the key events and people that have defined his life. This book is about him not me but it does bring back many of my memories of people and events from 1970 onwards. David tells the truth when he writes that even when you are "short with short legs for my height", if you work hard enough then you can find success in individual sports.

Books about people's athletics lives rarely get written, or if they do they never see the light of day. The stories tend to become folklore and only discussed in pubs after races!

David grew up near me in Hendon, North London, joined Shaftesbury Barnet Harriers (my lifelong club) and trained (maybe a little more slowly and less often) around the same routes that I did during my career, one of which was the wonderful Hampstead Heath. He remembers the club in the 1970's being known, not unfairly as "a Drinking Club with a Running Problem" because of its lively social life. The fact that he later joined Highgate Harriers was not as I understand it for their temperance values! His knowledge of athletics is impressive, and it is no surprise that he later moved into the world of coaching.

His stories of athletics in Kenya make interesting reading as does his candour about his ill-fated involvement in setting up a training camp there. This does not however appear to have spoilt his overall relationship with the country and its people and allows him insight that explains the impact of the benefits of being a good Kenyan runner and understanding why there seems to be a high number of athletes that risk taking drugs. David had some occasions as an athlete manager which makes interesting reading! Later Spanish athletics also gets its fair share of criticism amidst his enthusiasm. I am assuming that he has cleared his recollections with legal advice!

David talks honestly about the pressures that coaches come under from false allegations by their athletes, his views on coaches being paid and the resentment that athletes changing coaches can bring if not done sensibly. He is well read and talks about the murky side of athletics that he and others have experienced - something which is rarely mentioned.

David is a well-respected coach who has filled his life with running and coaching. Without people like him athletics and running would not exist!

Dave Bedford
Former 10,000 metres world record holder and London Marathon Race Director
June 2024

Introduction

Our sport is founded on many years and decades of personal and collective achievements and is also steeped in history, heritage, and pivotal moments that influence our lives.

Since our formation in 2006 England Athletics have introduced a Hall of Fame to symbolise the embracement of our rich history and heritage as a sport and have also initiated a wider heritage project, museum, and library project in partnership with our friends at the AAA, who prior to our inception held the responsibility for the governance in the sport. We have also recognised the efforts and achievements of many dedicated volunteer coaches, officials, and administrators in our sport through our annual volunteer awards programme.

At England Athletics we encourage people to talk openly about their experiences through their own lens and embrace the concept of recognising and acknowledging the past through the diversity of thought and in applying personal insights, learnings, and perspectives to help shape the future thinking and delivery of our sport in a positive way to benefit all. We feel it is important that personal views and opinions on our sport are collated and expressed to inform the future – and that we can learn much from the past to help shape the future whether that be positive, negative, or indifferent in terms of actions and practices. .

We were pleased and humbled to be asked by David to pen a few words for his book and congratulate him for taking the time to put his own thoughts down on paper based on his experiences, his views, and personal perspectives that he has on our great sport. As someone who has committed a great deal of time, energy, and dedication to our sport, particularly in the endurance events, we are sure that readers will find his personal accounts interesting and thought provoking. May it encourage those who read it to take their first steps into coaching and participation or to take up another role within our great diverse sport.

Chris Jones and Tom Craggs, England Athletics August 2024

PREFACE

Person A: "*I'm writing my next book.*"
Person B: "*Great, neither am I.*"

In these nine words of comic genius from the 1960s Peter Cook and Dudley Moore strike into one of the basic traits of the human condition. That is, if we have a task that we know is going to take a very long time, throw up numerous tough challenges and may not even produce a satisfying result when achieved, we will tend to delay completing it or indeed even starting it. Of course, without applying this urge to strive on, James Joyce stays in the Dublin pub and doesn't write "Ulysses", Baron Hausmann casually gazes out at the garden when he ought to be redesigning the centre of Paris as the City of Light, Kate Bush calls it a day at Grade 5 piano and Robert Oppenheimer just stays as a pretty canny mathematician who likes a good firework display.

So I can confidently state I've spent large amounts of time not writing this book although the idea of it has lazily remained, and in various forays of activity I have done the writing bit which is what follows.

And speaking of things that take a long time, throw up numerous tough challenges and may not even produce a truly satisfying result, there's running.

For many of us running can seem to be everything and it can also seem to be as nothing. To explain….for at least part of our lives, our running has dictated or at least influenced, our shape, our weight (though not, I will concede, our height); when we go to bed and when we get up; what, when and how much we eat and drink; who our friends and, maybe, our partners are; maybe even what jobs we do, or how we go about keeping on top of our jobs. On the other hand, nobody loves, hates, likes or dislikes us because we run; very rarely are we employed, or not, because of our running; and however much, and for however long, we are sucked into the world of running, there are people, places and experiences that matter hugely to us, and do so regardless of the running strand in our lives.

To allude to one dramatic example of where someone's running came to embody and represent so much more than the activity and the results, is the man who to many is seen as the greatest living Ethiopian, Haile Gebreselasie. He himself has said that if he were to stand as a presidential candidate, he would expect to win easily, but won't do so unless and until he can fulfil the demands of the role. In a land where extraordinary talented distance runners are numerous, he stands for so much more than what his running has achieved in the confines of the sport.

Never mind the celebrity status or material wealth that any Olympic running champion should, deservedly, acquire in their home nation, there are some for whom running has been an enabler to acquire some real power. So, for Finn Lasse Viren, Portuguese Rosa Mota, and Italian Alberto Cova. Olympic Gold helped them on the path to Parliamentary and even ministerial roles. Prodigious USA miler Jim Ryun wound up as a Kansas delegate to the USA Congress; Moroccan Olympic Hurdles Champion Nawal El Moutawakel became a global force in driving up the role and opportunities for women in athletics. Whilst closer to home Sebastian Coe found that a tremendously swift and winning set of races over 800 and 1500 metres helped open the doors to various corridors of real power. (In an early role he gave Personal Training sessions to then Conservative Leader of the Opposition William Hague so must at least have accessed his corridor albeit at that stage somewhat light on actual power).

The book is absolutely not intended to be a coaching guide for runners but it's possible that runners might find something in it that in some way helps them think about their running progress. Nor does it have any pretensions about being of practical benefit to coaches, but if you are a coach or thinking about shifting from running to coaching there may be something that may help at some stage. If you finish the book and you have found something that enhances your appreciation of what is an eternally fascinating, sometimes joyful yet sometimes cruel, whilst consistently fulfilling sport, at however profound or superficial a level, then that will be my justification for writing it.

There are as many runners' tales as there are runners. Here, set in the wide – and ever-widening - context of the last few decades of modern running, are some parts of mine.

A FEW MORE LAPS

1

THE YEARS BEFORE

My earliest actual memory is, bizarrely, from aged seven. It was at my cousins' house and was the very moment when England lost the World Cup. It's as close as sporting history seems to get to actual history within the national sporting psyche (Scottish readers are permitted to smirk knowingly here) and the details were that England were defending the World Cup won in 1966 (which you may be aware of, it has been mentioned occasionally in football writing in the last half century, although the Glasgow Herald cheekily logged it as Results In Brief) and had a tricky quarter final against West Germany. The trickiness quota was raised by the fact that the legendary goalkeeper Gordon Banks was injured and was replaced by the less rock-solid Peter Bonnetti. And so it panned out – with England's 2-0 lead being whittled away in the final minutes with German goal poacher Gerd Muller pouncing to help beat the defending champions 3-2 in extra time. At age seven the two specific things I remember – and neither of these were picked up in the following media punditry surrounding the match – were, firstly, we watched it in colour. This was great as it enabled viewers to readily pick out the Germans in their white shirts and black shorts. My cousins were early adopters of this wonderful new technology (colour TV, not monochrome sports kit), as part of their affluence, which reached such heights that they sometimes went on overseas holiday twice in the same year. Secondly, we watched the match with a guy called Sanjay who was on the stout side and I remember my grandfather calling him, to his face, 'tubby' as he asked him to move along a little to share the sofa.

The second memory carries somewhat less heft in the national sporting heritage but serves to show what cretins little boys can be. Some of us can, after many years, grow out of this phase, I have been told. My new-born cousin was just back from hospital in her cot and my elder cousin, aged nine, suggested we give her some early swearing lessons. We did actually use the words 'swearing lessons'. This was shortly after the World Cup defeat, so we were presumably at a loss on the football viewing front, and so there we stood, over a baby not yet a month old, uttering our choicest swear words to enable her to get a linguistic head start. So when, now in her early fifties, I hear her swear, which she only does very rarely under the most extreme stress and provocation of course, I feel a frisson of ownership of the outpoured oath.

Maybe it's a British post-Empire and European-stragglers thing – one's first memory being that England lost at football, at which they were, until the West Germans took the upper hand, the champions. Slightly before my memory, but ultimately far more profound than a quarter final of anything, the first major iconic sports moment in my lifetime, when sport was demonstrably making a mark far beyond the sport itself, came in October 1968. The photos of the medal ceremony for the Men's 200 metres in the Mexico City Olympics show the gold and bronze medallists, Tommie Smith and John Carlos of the USA, walking out sombrely wearing black socks, no shoes and as they climbed the podium, donning a single black shining glove on their hand which they raised as the Stars and Stripes flag climbed the flagpole. They faced down, not looking out at the flag or the audience or indeed the world's cameras. It's a devastating image and scenario; how at the moment of every athlete's dream, when they are justified, indeed expected, to be totally self-focused, these two runners chose to submerge their own achievements and draw the world's attention to something they thought far more fundamental than their own amazing speed around the track. The video footage is still transfixing.

The lack of any earlier memory is no doubt related to the catastrophe that my family went through. My father died suddenly when I was four.

He was thirty-four. So after the whole of my life so far, the total body of connections I have with my father amounts to a few seconds of reel-to-reel magnetic tape that my younger sister has caringly preserved of him recording whilst he played with us; a couple of birthday cards to and from him in the absurdly brief window that embraced me being able to understand the concept of a birthday card, and him being alive; and a picture of his grave on which the commemoration reads " A wonderful man with great compassion, vitality and humour who had so much to give to all who knew him". And that's it. So whatever normal people have within their minds and feelings towards their father, I have only a nothingness. As nothingness goes, it has a somewhat hefty unchanging presence throughout my very core. His school reports suggest that he had a maverick mischievous element, and a tendency to push against rules and accepted systems and my sister and I have similar traits.

Life unfolds and one can't always say why certain paths are followed, or not followed, but I think it very unlikely that I'd have taken to the strange activity of running with the dedication that I did if childhood had been something more traditionally normal. On a simple practical level, at about age 12 a family friend who was a surgeon suggested that I should have regular cardio check-ups and start some aerobic activity to keep my cardiovascular system in healthy shape. He may as well have dressed up as the Grim Reaper and come at me with a scythe for the galvanising effect this had, so almost from the next day I started to jog/walk, pretty much daily, staring with a breathless mile or so round our local streets and then, from this very low base, just building and building – with, at that very early stage, no mental connection between this 'survival ' fitness (as I saw it initially) and the sport of running which I followed only as a fan. After about 18 months I made the leap across. Almost a half century later, and now fully 20 years since I was what I consider an active runner, the very fundamental need to do something aerobic almost every single day, for an hour plus, to keep the cardio in working order is engrained in my life pattern.

Of other immediate family members in the same line, my father's sister is still going strong at 85, his elder brother lived until 89 and his own father, who was a stout little man who liked a cigar, saw out his life in largely good health until 86 years old, so my father had the uniquely worst of bad deals. We never, absolutely never, talk about this in the family, at least no one does when I'm present. I wouldn't know what to say or indeed if there is anything at all I could offer to say. So everything that follows is, one way or another, trying to make some sort of order and sense from a fractured start. T.S Eliot, in 'East Coker', captures some fundamental truths that one way or another we all go through in life, at varying levels of intensity and awareness. I'd suggest that anyone who puts themselves through the mill in the tough unforgiving sport of distance running is definitely taking the thornier of the available paths.

"To arrive where you are, to get from where you are not,
  You must go by a way wherein there is no ecstasy.
  In order to arrive at what you do not know
  You must go by a way which is the way of ignorance.
  In order to possess what you do not possess
  You must go by the way of dispossession.
  In order to arrive at what you are not
  You must go through the way in which you are not."

That is, whatever you are, you have some inner feeling and thought that there is something else you'd like to experience and become. You aren't sure quite what it is or will feel like, but you feel the deep urge to do whatever and end up wherever. Of course, religion is the most obvious experiential path that 'fits' this but it needn't be.

Childhood rolled... on and my first attendance at an athletics event came, with great excitement, aged nine. I made the long trek across London to Crystal Palace with a schoolmate and his mum to watch the long since defunct Southern Counties International events. This was the last main domestic meeting before the Munich Olympics, in the summer of 1972. The stars I caught sight of – and cherished autographs from - at the time, included the likes of Alan Pascoe, Sonia Lannaman, Andrea Lynch, and David Jenkins – all major championship medallists and high achieving Olympians. The autographical highlights were David Hemery, then at his peak and Great Britain's only defending gold medallist from the 1968 Mexico City Games. The gap between star athletes and fans was far less demarcated than it is today and once the race was run, it was simple to move over the walls onto the area between stands and trackside. I don't remember what happened to keep over enthusiastic viewers from intruding on the track itself but there was definitely a closeness that is no longer available at this level. Another coveted (or should that be cOVETTed) signature and indeed endurance memory was seeing Steve Ovett aged 17 run a sub 4 minute mile – indeed he matched Roger Bannister's iconic 3.59.4. Even aged ten I was aware that running sub 4 aged 17, whilst still what we used to call a 6th former, was phenomenal. I also was struck that as a 17-year-old Ovett had an impressive beard and tremendously powerful and developed physique. One signature I acquired where the athlete's subsequent life perhaps shone more brightly than his impressive track pedigree was 400 metre runner Roger Jenkins. He was a Scotland and GB rep, World Student Games medallist but never quite the match of his more prodigious younger brother David. In his mid-50s Roger Jenkins moved, with a 35-year gap, from the footnotes in the sports columns to occasional prominence in the financial pages with details of his staggering income and wealth accrued working for Barclays Capital. He was at one stage one of the UK's highest salaried employees.

My first recollections of watching televised elite athletics had an early and very ugly exposure to the political links that international sport brings. It was the 1972 Munich Olympics and the track and field programme, and indeed the entire Games, were torn apart by the Black September terrorist group breaking into the Israeli apartments in the athletes' village and killing nine people. Renowned athletics commentator David Coleman was given the unenviable task (this sort of event in later years would surely never have been handled by a sports specialist) of providing the news coverage for the BBC as the slaughter unfolded. I vaguely recall mixed feelings as I was just getting into the events and the killings happened in the middle of the track programme. The athletics timetable carried on pretty much as scheduled, after much debate on what was a suitable way forward for the Games, and amidst all the specific track events the Games went down in the bigger picture of history for this terrible violation of what sport was supposedly meant to inspire.

At the time it seemed a reasonable position to state, at least from the perspective of a country outside the then Soviet Union and its Warsaw Pact satellite nations, that politics should be kept separate from sport. Whilst we didn't quite go back to the ancient Greek Olympic paradigm whereby wars supposedly stopped during the Games, within the world of amateur sport and still barely one generation since the second World War, it seemed that war was part of a separate strand of life from sport.

Half a century later this apolitical notion of sport would just seem hugely naive and ill informed. With the growth of public awareness of soft power; the increasing sports washing trend of repressive states mainly but not only in the Arab world; and the vast sums spent by national and city governments in hosting sports events and then funding their elite sports people, sport has become almost as political as, say, policies on education or welfare benefits or transport. (As an illustration that covers all these aspects, details of the operating costs for some recent Winter Olympic hosts were Lillehammer 1994 $1 billion; Salt Lake City 2002 $2 billion; Torino 2006 $0.7 billion, Vancouver 2010 1.7 $billion; 2014 Sochi $51 billion. Sochi was the same winter as the Russian incursion into Ukraine. However, the kleptocrats' jamboree at Sochi didn't buy permanent Olympic merriment as Russia was banned from the Olympics in December 2019 because of its state-managed pan-sport doping programme. Now that's political.)

I discovered early on that the annoying thing about athletics was that I wasn't any good at it and never likely to become so either. Relatively short and with short legs for my height, a family tendency to put on weight around the backside and thighs, poor coordination, and with no great skill acquisition across the sporting menu (though I did become quite proficient at table tennis, though nowhere near good enough to get a book's worth of material from the sport). What I gradually picked up, in my early to mid-teens, was that, at a reasonable club sort of level, if you hadn't been born with some ability to run fast, then you had no chance at sprinting. For longer events, if you were determined enough to put in the effort and put some sensible structure around the effort, then you could become competent at longer distances in particular. It's hard to pinpoint one's motivations and stimuli so many years ago, at an age slightly pre-adolescence (and my adolescence kicked in somewhat later than the aforementioned Ovett's) but I do recall that whilst I was competent and reasonably diligent at most aspects of traditional schoolwork, what I really tried my hardest at was sport, and particularly any individual sport.

At age eleven I took to writing down all the athletics medallists from the 1974 European Championships and Commonwealth Games. I can't recall why I did this as the practical benefits, even with over 45 years hindsight, aren't clear. Perhaps I had a nice Parker pen I was keen to flourish, although my appalling handwriting doesn't really sit well with 'flourish'. The medal data wasn't something you could trot out with your mates to get some lively banter going, ('What did you think of Karl Honz running that 45.3 400 metres for West Germany?' was never going to be the coolest playground ice breaker. Even, I suspect, in West Germany). I still recall that I was meticulous about getting full details on the track results and if a couple of minutiae from the less glamourous field events slipped my 11-year-old eye for detail, well it seemed not quite so crucial. Maybe I'm retrofitting my memories, 1 but I think that even then I thought that there were more throwing events than strictly necessary, and that Pole Vault seemed just superfluous. We had high jump already, why did some zealous innovator have to say 'Yes that's fine but what about if we make you use a stick for some extra oomph over the bar'). Think about it – Pole Vault is the only event in the entire track and field programme that has two different extraneous items to be carried out – it's just too busy to be as pure as the other events. (Pedants – including myself – are now tying ourselves in knots over whether the water jump in the steeplechase is a different item from the hurdles).

I'm sure these early forays were essential in instilling a great enthusiasm as a fan of track and field athletics (all four words being the key, though probably there's not much resonance in the word "and") rather than just endurance running. Running was the only discipline I pursued within the sport but I've always followed the sport across the events and it's only reluctantly that I may describe myself as a "running coach" rather than the preferred "athletics coach".

I accept the latter might run the risk of being approached to drill the finer points (or indeed any points) of discus or sprint hurdling though in twenty years of coaching that hasn't yet occurred. I think I know more about all the non-endurance events in track and field than I do about any other non-endurance sport. Though disappointingly this falls short of being offered a hammer throwing punditry role by the BBC. I apply every April, allowing good time to get all the key stats on board before the summer season gets rolling, but still no joy. I believe the main blockage is my unwillingness to relocate to Salford. This year, aware of the high-profile pressures on justifying the licence fee, I pitched on a BOGOF basis to cover discus as well, but sadly the same response.

So, throughout this book you'll notice that I switch between the world of endurance running and the world of athletics when the higher level machinations of the sport are relevant, because they are usually relevant to the sharper end of endurance running.

The downside of the "running coach" descriptor is that in the minds of some. this shades into Personal Trainer and thus they see me as someone who might meet them in St James Park at 6 a.m for some glute bridges and barefoot running drills before they head home for a kale and ginger smoothie. They say everyone has their price and, to avoid any clouding of roles, mine, for this, would be 50 per cent more than anyone would ever offer.

So, please, store this on the Athletics section of your bookshelf. Even if (especially if) this is the first item in that section. And now I'm off to meet my pole-vault conversion therapist.

2

SCHOOLBOY ERRORS

By the 1976 Olympics in Montreal, I had of course worked out the infantile futility of this pointless record keeping and moved on. Moved on, that is, to listing the Top 30 singles when they were announced every Wednesday at 12.30. This too may sound like a not especially dynamic youth pursuit but in my defence, I was embroiled in Bar Mitzvah classes at the time, so the bar of pre-teen excitement was not that high. Honestly, if you have ever tried reading Hebrew without the vowel indicators, when all the boys are out playing football or watching TV, it really starts to get exciting to learn whether The Damned are above or below Chic in the charts.

At secondary school, whilst in the first couple of years the chubby thighs and arse scenario was still prevalent, I was always keen to hear how the school's cross-country teams had got on and how they fared in the 800 and 1500 metres in summer track events. This was in the London Borough of Barnet, which has always had a particular niche in distance running, closely linked with the local Shaftesbury Barnet club. When I was ten, local man Dave Bedford set a world record at 10,000 metres. He had been to the local comprehensive, Whitefields (to where at my primary school, just across the A41 from this school, I was told that if I didn't get myself into a grammar school, I would be banished, to a supposed hotbed of teenage pregnancies. As a pipsqueak ten-year-old I was somewhat tangential on any pregnancy-related data set). Anyway, Bedford was raised less than a mile from where I was and had done many many miles of hill reps on the moderate local gradients between Golders Green and Cricklewood. (By coincidence he was in the same Whitefields school year as Tony Currie who had a long and illustrious career in professional football, his midfield skills deployed for the likes of Leeds United and Queens Park Rangers, both leading clubs, and including 17 caps for England). He had also done huge mileage around Hampstead Heath, one of London's wonderful green lungs. The club (men only – that's a sign of the times) also had close links with Barnet Ladies and Parkside (both for women only – you get the picture), for whom Joyce Smith achieved extraordinary long-distance success as women's racing distances gradually lengthened. In some subliminal way even before I was running, I felt inspired that these giants of the sport were putting in the work so locally.

The schoolboy star in Barnet in my year was Paul Simons and in light of later years it is amusing to recall the awed reverence with which I absorbed how he had dominated the local leagues, always winning by large margins. Now he is a friend of some 45 years standing and when we greet each other, whatever I display it would not be construed as awed reverence. Paul's bests as an adult were just over 30 minutes for 10k and a 2.23 marathon achieved in winning the now defunct Harrow marathon in his former Northwest London haunts. Now resident in Northwest England he has held two marathon world bests for fancy-dress guises including 2.55 decked out as Father Christmas and when he was 50 the hugely coveted prize of world's fastest water bottle, clocking 3.30. In answer to the inevitable question about whether he trained in the required kit, the answer is no, though the water bottle regalia does secure him a seat on a busy train. However, he finds the whole airport security thing tiresome, with officers assessing whether he is more or less than 100 millilitres. At a pinch he would trade these world bests for a UK record in standard attire. In later years he has done sterling service as a pacer for numerous UK and overseas marathons, his pacing allocation slipping a little as he ages. At time of writing, he is in delicate negotiations for pacing the 6 hours 30 group (yes, that is correctly written) at a world major which will be more a test of attention span than aerobic prowess.

My own novice running, when I was motivated to start some running rather than just gawp at the achievements of others, was actually as much about losing weight, showing independence from a rather protective mother and grandma, as it was about performance ambitions. And, of course, if you fancy getting better at running, actually doing some tends to be a useful way of getting the ball rolling. The big step was at age 14 presenting myself at the Shaftesbury Novices Cross Country race. Slowness progressed to mediocrity which progressed to.....well, actually that's about all I ever achieved, at least within the highly competitive environments in which I was involved. I recall the first time, as an adult, I checked the International Amateur Athletics Federation (IAAF – the world governing body which later rebranded as World Athletics) endurance training manuals, their various guidelines and tables showed performance data only down to the level of my approximate personal bests at 10k and marathon. I assume the rationale was that if you take the sport, and your training, at all seriously, seriously enough that the IAAF actually recognised you as part of its sport, rather than some well- meaning but talent-free short termer, then you must, surely, be able to get to these levels as a bare minimum. On reflection, that was a rationale not out of line with how some Harrier clubs operated although they wouldn't word it quite like that.

From a very early stage I was acquainted with the drop out out trend in youth sport. I could never understand these guys' motivation, or lack of. I thought it was a great weekend agenda to get the homework sorted, come over all sullen and monosyllabic with my mum (actually, that endearing trait was an ongoing weekly pattern, it didn't really have any particular weekend focus), then go out to cross country races most Saturdays and get hammered by more talented runners, returning home for supper and with just enough time and energy to row with my sister over her borrowing my Stranglers LPs without my permission or any sort of hire charge. I had offered her a 10% family reduction, as you can't really rip off your own sibling, but more than clawed this back with a 20% between-the-bedrooms delivery charge as we got on badly at the time.

And yet some – the vast majority, over time - of these talented athletes decided as they went through their teens to pack in their participation. What could they do on a Saturday afternoon that was better than doing a sport they were really good at? There was a worrying trend that within Shaftesbury as I made my snail-like progress, as and when I beat the next runner up the rankings in a race, he would simply stop doing the sport. It wasn't an official governing body rule, or formalised in the club's constitution, that if I beat you, you had to leave the sport in humiliation, but it seemed to pan out like that.

The talent in the local area was prodigious – my first nondescript run in the Northwest London League also marked the club debut of one Gary Staines, of Verlea in Welwyn Garden City. He went on to run two Olympic Games finals at 5,000 metres, at which event he was a European Championship silver medallist. You can guess whose debut stirred up more comments at the post race tea urn. Just a few miles further East around the not-yet-existing M25 in Enfield was Steve Crabb, who went on to run 3.51 for one mile and compete for Britain at 1500 metres at the World Championships. At national level there was the long-distance poetry in motion of Cornish runner Jon Richards. I still maintain that he was the most talented junior UK-born distance runner I've seen in my lifetime and some of the statistics bear this out. For some decades he held UK Age records for 3k and 5k in the 16-18 age groups. As context to quite how fast he was, Mo Farah was already standing out as a tremendous talent at this age and stage, and his own best times at that age don't match what Richards achieved. At national level, he would typically win Championships at Cross country by over a minute over around four miles of racing – so, he was about 4% or 5% faster than the next best British runner, and this in an era when there were some super young talents in the sport. He was so good that a very distant second best in the age group in the county, and indeed his own club, Duchy of Cornwall, was his club mate Dave Buzza who went on to run for GB with a 2.11 marathon and 62 half marathon. That double z in the surname is always a good indicator of Cornish lineage. Triple z just indicates you've nodded off.

I always used to wonder, whatever else these dropout runners do in life, it is extremely unlikely that they will ever be as good at anything else as they were at running, so why didn't they just defer the 'anything else' part of life that bit longer. With age and experience, I have come to see the other side from the talented runner's perspective. Just because you have great talent at something, (it could be any sport or music – how many of us know people who zipped through Grades 1 to 8 by their mid-teens and then gave up at a stroke?) it doesn't guarantee that that you will like doing the activity. With distance running this imbalance between ability and love of the sport may be particularly potent – it's highly time consuming, has a big knock-on effect on time and simply spare energy for other things, has very slim odds of earning any remuneration, and there will always be someone better than you.

I'm sure that the mind-set of many of these youthful stars is different than the rest of us – they can have realistic ambitions of running in the Olympics for a few years, until gradually it may become apparent that they may never be quite good enough. From that perspective, winning local or even regional 10ks, maybe even running for your country at some minor level, may just not seem worth the candle when you have set your sights on the stars.

I lived almost exactly at the mid-way point between the Shaftesbury HQ at Copthall stadium in Mill Hill and Highgate Harriers' base at Parliament Hill track. Both had plentiful fields around the track. There was no particular reason why I chose Shaftesbury though I was aware of their biggest names more than I knew of any Highgate speedster.

The earliest actual coached sessions I did were with stalwart Bryan Smith though there was not understood to be any individual attention. The Tuesday evening (some things never change) session was built primarily for his wife, the pioneering Joyce Smith who after a starry career at 1500m and then 3000m was in the later years of her peak hacking into the British marathon record culminating, in her early 40s, in two runs at 2.29 to win the earliest London marathons plus several other major marathons at what was then the sharp end of world class. The group sessions were fairly standard sets of 400s, 800s, 1200s and 1600s. As it happened, I was, by about age 19, very evenly matched with Joyce over these sort of efforts although you won't find any reports disclosing how Joyce used to benefit from hanging onto my coattails of a Tuesday at 6.30pm. Only many years later did I learn from Bryan that Joyce would do these sessions after a fairly brisk 8 or 9 miles the same morning at not far shy of 6 minute miling. That goes some way to explaining why she was knocking out 2.29s and I wasn't. It was a nice evenly matched little group with very little "spread " of ability in how we paced these sessions.

At local level the mid-teen prodigy was David Sweeney, who, with his Anglo-Irish roots, went to St James Catholic High, in the Burnt Oak/Colindale area which at the time had a strong Irish contingent. At the time this was a tough school though it's not true that Dave became outrageously fit just to run away from local hard nuts. More athletically relevant, the suburb was a very neat warm up jog distance from Copthall stadium. He was competing at the highest national level – one standout race I recall, and which four decades later would still have a wow factor at any local schools' event anywhere in the world outside Kenya or Ethiopia, was the Borough Schools Champs 5,000. On what was a very windy evening, and totally solo from the gun, Dave powered round 5000m, aged 17, in 14.33, just to show he was best in our Borough. Over 40 years later, Dave recalls "I decided that that year I would try and leave an indelible mark in the record books." And he emphatically did so. Yours truly was runner up but I may as well as have been on another planet as in the same race, over two minutes in arrears. It's a very poignant moment when Dave digs up his detailed handwritten training log from all these years back and sends over the screenshot. The diary refers to the cold and the wind and mentions with no irony that he decided to front run this one – as if there was any other realistic option. Notable also is that just four days prior he had run two 10 mile efforts, and even the day before had done a steady 12 miles. Within a few months we would hear of the extraordinary Loughborough University set up he had joined – at least a dozen notably quicker guys, including a certain post-graduate Sebastian Coe who made his presence known in the sporting world one way or another. Sweeney also had some state-of-the-art green and yellow Adidas SL76 trainers though I never know if there was a causal link between his performance and his footwear.

I was extremely shy at the time – and, ridiculous as it now seems, I was almost too intimidated to even to speak to Dave, a club-mate, unless spoken to. Ditto age-group club-mate and another lean and driven fastie Phil Llewellyn, who had the extra cachet of having run for Wales in the World Cross Country Championships, though his Potters Bar lineage and accent didn't show the most obvious kinship with Owen Glendower or the Men of Harlech.

To indicate what might have been for Dave at his peak ages, after marrying an Australian woman and building a successful life in Queensland, he became fully immersed in his training in his mid 40s and as he went through the next 15 years he was regularly trading Australian age group records at 5k and 10k with legendary compatriot and one year younger Steve Moneghetti. The latter had a wonderful senior career, numerous world class results and medals across track, road and cross country including a 2.08 Berlin marathon win (the iconic race in the year the Berlin Wall had come down) amongst others and a World Champs bronze at marathon. Catching up online at 20,000 kilometres distance with the 2024 version, Dave updates "Today I am in one of those noncompeting phases. I run every day; I am on a 5 year streak. I think competitively I achieved all I wanted to after winning those 4 Masters World Championships in Perth so when the body started to slow me down, I felt no competitive drive to race."

Two particular races at Parliament Hill stand out from these bygone years. One has been chronicled down the years since 1981 when Shaftesbury top dog Julian Goater won the 9-mile National cross country by a staggering one minute and fifty-five seconds. As context, this was as ever the trial for the World Championships and at this stage, before the East Africans really joined the party, the England team (Home Countries sent their own teams at this date) was invariably among the world's best and was peppered with sub 28-minute 10,000 metre guys. As such, a 20 to 30 second national win was treated as hugely dominant. As I watched Goater through the drizzle on his day of days I became totally convinced that he had been misdirected along the course, missed a loop somewhere and would thus have to be disqualified.

The second race that stuck in my memory as a spectator, and

coincidentally the lead role was another Shaftesbury runner, came some 20 years later. It was the English Schools cross country championship senior boys' race, the winner of which can justifiably be considered the best male distance runner in the entire population of the nation's schools. Making the most of this opportunity, the runner grabbing the national glory was almost literally racing in his own back yard. Representing Middlesex, Richard Williams was a pupil at Highgate school, and as you leave the top end of Parliament Hill and Kenwood you simply cross the road and you are at the entry to Highgate school's playing fields. On a lovely sunny early spring day the local harrier had a commanding lead by half way and as I watched I wondered what he might do in the sport to surpass this moment. Whilst many county teams had very long return journeys north or west, he could just about do his warm down jog to traipse to the shower at home near Muswell Hill. He then went to Bristol University and one way or another never rose to these heights. He became a teacher (like his father and coach Geoff, an inspiring and insightful guy whom I only got to know later in life) and perhaps unsurprisingly coaches a cross-country team at his school in Hertfordshire.

Individuals aside, the Parliament Hill fields venue is great for gaining a strong impression of just how fit the best international level runners are. As you walk over the fields you cannot help but notice how hilly the terrain is and, invariably, how heavy underfoot it is, whether muddy and wet or dry and clumpy or often a mixture of both (there's a fuller section detailing the tricky trends of north London soil drainage, which commercial pressures have obliged me to syndicate to Geologists Monthly) the speed at the sharp end of the big races seems to defy the toughness of the ground they are ploughing through.

There was at this time, prior to the very late 1970s, almost no 'fun running' – the only relatively slower runners were a few older guys (far fewer older women) who had previously been quicker, never left the sport and had slowed with age. You wouldn't really find men running 10ks slower than about 40 minutes – people did athletics as a competitive sport, which meant that you trained pretty much daily, or you didn't do it in any structured way at all. The changes started happening pretty rapidly around the turn of the 1970s to the 1980s. Most of the reasons have been documented elsewhere. I suspect that deep down there was a subconscious drive to run around in circles until exhaustion as a displacement activity, because the two main national political options were either a Labour Government giving the country away to the International Monetary Fund or what would soon be known as Thatcherism. (There was also the National Front party though that arguably was more about unlicenced combat sport than politics). Running 100 miles per week numbed the pain though the rampant inflation did unfortunately mean that the cost of your Sunday roast went up about 5% between when you headed out the door for the weekly long run and when you came back to eat it.

A huge crew of new adult and veteran (over 40) runners would soon make me look, by comparison, a little less feeble. In 1981 I did a Junior (Under 20) cross country race where in a field of about fifty just three runners finished behind me. Within a year, despite the best efforts of some top-notch psychologists to restore them with some vestiges of self-esteem, all three had felt obliged to emigrate to South America and assume new identities. I was around about a sub 17-minute 5k runner at that time – put that into parkrun today and....you get the picture of how the sport has become so much more inclusive. Four months later, just before turning eighteen, I ran my first marathon. Called the People's Marathon it was held in Solihull, a leafy suburb of Birmingham, a few weeks after the first ever London Marathon. I finished in 42nd place out of some 2000 finishers, clocking 2 hours 42 minutes. I wasn't even the first 17-year-old – an even more endurance-driven fellow from Leamington knocked out the distance in 2.27. He wasn't known as a particularly topflight runner at the standard Junior distance events, as context to what else was going on in the competitive world of harrierdom.

As for school itself, one of the particular traits was that it was something of a shoplifting school. Not in any formal sense – the school brochure didn't state 'We offer a wide traditional curriculum, with many boys moving on to leading Universities. Outside the core curriculum we have a strong sporting ethos, particularly basketball and cricket; and a thriving cadet corps for those who hit adolescence and still find guns and marching around a playground in khaki fascinating. For those wishing to explore the boundaries of legality and how the retail world works in practice, a sizable posse of boys steal from local shops, an enticing range of which are handily appointed to fill in the daily lunch break'. No, it wasn't like that, but for whatever reason the school year above and below mine and indeed my year itself, did have a big group of boys who went through a stage where shoplifting became just another activity, like sport, reading, or photography, albeit when listing our interests to potential pen friends we kept this pastime under wraps. I say 'we' because for a while I was somewhat entrenched in this. I write this aware that Clare Balding has put on record her own shoplifting experience and that has not prevented her becoming an official National Treasure.

At the top end of the school pilfering CV was – allegedly – one lad who had apparently used wire cutters to make a hi-fi shop somewhat lighter in stock than its inventory would otherwise show. When we small timers heard about this we had two thoughts. Firstly, it might not have been true and secondly, if it was, we weren't going to head down that level of retail therapy. And even the bulkiest of 1977 parkas couldn't really conceal a hi-fi unit.

Perhaps predictably, the one local confectionery outlet that you really couldn't nick from was the school tuck shop, where a wire mesh shield had been precisely set up so as to exactly fit around the display trays, managed by prefects. Maybe it's a false memory but in my mind's eye I think I see some 12- and 13-year-olds desperately trying to pick at the extremes of the wire barrier to snaffle a Frys Chocolate Cream to ease their (alright then, our) nutritional strategy through that awkward mid-morning lull.

The two occasions when I was found out are worth relating, – a nuanced combination of sensing the correct moral path, pragmatism, and adolescent fear. Not necessarily in that order, though I think I should get the moral factor in early doors. The first time was something I never fully worked out. My old school friend (we'll rename him Andrew so as not to jeopardise his continued role at the Supreme Court) was somehow rumbled by his mum that he had nicked a packet of chewing gum. Given that our weekly pocket money covered maybe four packs of chewing gum I never quite worked out what led to this 'J'accuse' scenario and his own confession, and implication of myself. His mum was a Liberal council member, so I'd assume not so likely to use the less ethical methods of interrogation. At least, not on her son. So my mother confronted me and I too had to confess to the same offence as he had. At the time my bookshelves were gradually filling up with numerous volumes of Mad Books and Billy Bunter acquired similarly so I thought that if my mum was so freaked out by a clandestine pack of Wrigley's Juicy Fruit gum I should most definitely keep the books out of the equation.

The other occasion was at a WH Smiths. It was the first time I was ever caught within a store and – predictably but thankfully – the last time I ever tried to take anything. The item in question was a 7-inch single record, a vaguely bohemian song 'Imagine Me, Imagine You' by Fox. The manager walked up to me and my accomplice and said we needed to come back to his office and he'd arrange for us to pay for the items. It was very chastening although I did calculate that paying the recommended retail price for a single I actually wanted was not so bad an outcome. My friend did likewise – though as his record was the ghastly 'comedy' song Funky Gibbon by The Goodies his own financial risk management seemed altogether much poorer. This was all before I had started any running – though I think it's a stretch to suggest that the discovery of aerobic endeavours diverted me from a potential life of criminality. The later career paths of the juvenile thieves included a BBC producer (who, just maybe, might have had a chance to compare past escapades with Ms Balding), a General Medical Practitioner, an award winning Director of Photography in the film industry, a Professor of English and, ironically, two chaps who work in book retailing and have to face the corporate exasperation of stolen books.

In my Year 10 we joined with a local comprehensive – not just any comprehensive but a really challenged one ('challenged' would absolutely not have been the word we used at the time), with many boys from vastly different backgrounds from the majority of us. It was quite a transformation, and literally overnight. Well, not quite that literally,

UK bureaucracy doesn't really do things overnight, and in the relevant year of 1978 most of the UK workforce was on a picket line anyway so hardly available to merge two schools at great haste. It was done over the summer holidays but with no transition or pilot phase.

In a horribly insensitive way that with hindsight I find surprising that it was how things worked in the late 1970s, there was a notable discrepancy between the boys who were given out a weekly series of school lunch tickets, and those boys who were then called up to actually pay for the meals. What I remember was that at age 14 to 15 there were guys from this new intake who were almost totally absent from school – just names on the register who showed up maybe once per week, on which days they sat there in almost total miserable silence. Sympathetic liberal chaps as we were, we created a nickname for our new school colleagues. We were quite a thoughtful bunch so the collective was to use the name of their old school followed by the word 'scum'. Our feeble 'wordplay' was counterpoised by our cowardice as we would never use this word to any of the boys' faces – or we would risk having our own rearranged for the worse.

Two incidents sum up the polarised nature of the combination of the two schools. Those of us doing O level Latin had our lessons in the same class as those in the same year who did what was then called Remedial Studies and examples of both groups' work was put on the walls. So – and you don't know whether to laugh or weep at this – on one wall you could peruse some smartarses's word perfect translation of a scene from Caesar's Gallic Wars, whilst on the adjacent wall you could admire how someone else had learned to write a sentence about his cat. Perhaps an even starker contrast, there was a little Oxbridge tutorial group led by our head of 6th form to, just maybe, help people not make complete laughing stocks of themselves in the Oxbridge general entrance exam. The group met weekly, though one week the session was cancelled because the teacher had to go and support one of the new intake of scu.... boys who was being charged with rape (for which he was subsequently convicted). We were aware of why the teacher was absent and it was so far beyond our experience that we didn't really know how to articulate whatever bemusement we felt.

One of the quirks of my year group was that five boys gained places to read maths at Cambridge. That was five more than was usual for the school. I was woefully out of my depth in classes with these guys and after about three minutes, when the bewildering display of squiggles, symbols and brackets on the blackboard had lost me, I just clocked out. When these boffins were on a roll it was like an astonishing spectator sport. Though as spectator sports go, Finchley Teens Do Hard Maths doesn't readily bear comparison with the Wimbledon singles final or the Real Madrid vs Barcelona match.

One notable runner who pitched up at my school but about four years below mine became something of a ground breaker. Of Kenyan birth I believe his family migrated to India and he arrived in London after a further trans-continental migration, with negligible English and so joined the first year at secondary school. Tall and very muscular for his purported age he very soon excelled at running, to the extent that he won the Middlesex schools cross country against boys up to 2 or more years older (years 7 to 9 in current terms). Then extraordinarily he won the English schools' championships too. The first and surely only time that a boy from this year group has done so. At this age a 2-year age gap is immense in terms of physical development. The following year he won again, still with a year in hand. And then in an unprecedented triple he won by a large margin in his top year at 14 to 15 years old. Notably though, his muscular shape remained very similar as two years prior as did his height so that amongst his school year group he was maybe average height. He notched up a similarly outstanding series of track performances from 800 to 3000 metres. He seemed to go off the radar from about Year 11. I think the probability is that his chronological age was 3 or 4 years ahead of the school year to which he was initially allocated, presumably because he had to start at the youngest year group whilst he got to grips with English. He was a popular and fairly quiet guy and we'll never know quite what thoughts he had as he notched up these astonishing results in his earliest years in London.

Our Head of Sixth form, who, for the right sort of person, was a genuinely inspirational teacher and highly witty man, with a great understanding of

16 to 18 year old males – had made it clear that if we were serious about our literary pretensions (and I use that last word advisedly in many cases, think in terms of purple velvet jackets with a Milan Kundera title just peeking over the top, though I owned no velvet of any hue, nor any East European novels) we should be hoovering up literature and pretty much side-lining other interests accordingly. Worryingly, these other interests would, in his mind, have included trying to run about 45 to 55 miles per week, studying Athletics Weekly and trying to hunt down affordable copies of the obscure early Alice Cooper albums before School's Out took him from the avant garde to megastardom. Mind you, he (our teacher, not Mr Cooper whose non-musical waking hours were split between obsessive consumption of beer and golf) also said that dyslexia was 'a disease invented by middle class parents whose kids are too thick to learn how to read' so he wasn't necessarily at the forefront of modern educational thinking. He was clearly conservative with both a small c and a big C. Indeed I expect some of the undiagnosed dyslexic guys who stretched his tolerance thought he was something of a C word though I don't know how they would have spelled it.

Other formative highlights from our Head of 6th form? Before the days when the former Polytechnics were reclassified as Universities, he was the teaching lead in the UCCA (now UCAS) Uni admission process. His baseline was 'If you are really keen simply to get into University, apply to Ulster' which in 1980-82, with the IRA on the prowl, was probably not one of the most Must See places in the UK for those wishing to reach adulthood with a full complement of working kneecaps. He also gave some grief to a friend who on the 'Other Interests' section had declared 'Sports except Horse Racing'. The sage pastoral advice was that unless he had some deep-seated moral problem with equine contests, he should simply keep the sporting interests at a generic level. One annoying fellow put 'Girls' in this section. Presumably at this stage of life he was just hugely relieved that although he hadn't been close to ever Doing It, he had tortuously worked out that when he did start Doing It, it would only be with girls, and so no fraught emotive family dialogues would be needed. He became a partner in one of London's top law firms and his partnership website profile majors on his other competencies.

The niceties of A Level markings in 1981 showed that after two years and hundreds of lessons my spoken French skills ('skills' a poor choice there, 'incapacity' more apt) had actually fallen from the mediocrity of the prior O Level. So don't necessarily assume that a learning curve always has some sort of upward trend. I had done quite well on the literature though. So if you wanted to get a toasted butty and a coffee anywhere between Ashford International and the Pyrenees, I was pretty much a dead loss. If, on the other hand, (au contraire, oh, we are rolling now) you wanted a couple of paragraphs, in English, on the fraught small-town tensions in some 19th century Corsican short stories, I could cobble it together.

We also had an enigmatic teacher who was perhaps metrosexual before it had been invented. He turned up once where a combination of some tight jeans, a worn-out patch around the ermm mid groin area, and one assumes that he had just used his last pair of undies the previous day because, was it a section of tentpole or......let's just say that if an Ofsted inspection had assessed him as 'Outstanding' there could be more than one interpretation of this. He did however have to deal with one rather pathetic academic howler I put my name to in our A Level mocks. I had never really been that interested in the animal world or anything military. So, at the time I knew that a 'cormorant' was a very large bird, kind of like an albatross, and I knew that a 'commodore' was....ah, well that was the thing. Do you know what a commodore is? Without googling? On the day in question, I just could not fathom that a commodore was anything other than a cormorant. Awkwardly, the text we had to critique was an extract centred on the village church wedding ceremony of a nice English lass and a cormor....errm a commodore. So off I headed into a load of irrelevance about the inexplicable anomaly of this peaceful idyllic pastoral scene having a massive-spanned seabird centre stage at the nuptials. I was so far off the literary pace at the time that I didn't even lob in a reference to 'magical realism' which might have scraped a mark for a woefully misguided but valiant straw-clutching try. In my defence, if a schoolboy, not yet 17, is poring over the contents of Athletics Weekly every seven days and ploughing through an extensive canon of fenced Billy Bunter books, perhaps he doesn't have the spare time to mug up on the officer hierarchy of the Royal Navy.

So, for the fearful Oxford interview, I had set off from home having just been shocked to hear the news from New York that John Lennon had been murdered a few hours earlier. I flagged up Agatha Christie and Frederick Forsyth as my main off-syllabus 'literature'. I think that the reply to the more probing question of 'Why?' brought forth some mumbled banality about plot and meticulous research. Something like a clued up 12-year-old could have done. With hindsight I should have pleaded that a case of Rock Fan PTSD had triggered my intellectual vacancy and that if the day had remained a normal Still Four Living Beatles Day, I'd have cut the literary mustard.

3

STRESS FRACTURE (DARK) BLUES

From a running point of view the Dreaming Spires was in my case more a city of Recurrent Stress Fractures. Not surprisingly, the University doesn't major on injured club runners whose aims of making running progress in a very handy environment are serially scuppered by metatarsal injuries and who instead 'invest' time in highly subsided lager. On the latter, I'm not sure if hindsight makes me more amazed at paying 50p for a pint or that I actually liked Foster's lager.

Whilst Universities, sensibly and naturally, make great play of their sporting success stories, of which there are many, there are also many disappointments. In the harder physiological sports, key factors are that the undergraduate age span is in many cases four years, itself a wide range between a young 18-year-old and a mature 22-year-old, and the age range is extended somewhat further when postgraduates are factored in. So the 18 year old fresher can be pitched against the 26 year old PhD student, and yet 3k or 5k or 6 miles cross country is the same distance for both. So there is the tendency that the fastest oldest runners (also of course they are usually the most experienced and often the most confident and persuasive) set the norm and the rest follow if they have the will – but the will is often unmatched by the physical robustness to support it. A full generation later I have had coaching experience with undergrad runners who have suffered similar injury cycles at university.

Anyway, it had its upside. Never having to get up in the morning to go training meant, well, never having to get up in the morning. There were occasional 9 a/m tutorials and it's bizarre how that nine o' clock appointment to be somewhere a five-minute cycle away seemed like a crack-of-dawn wake up call.

It's probably apparent that I hadn't been selected by the University to boost the Dark Blues sporting prowess. I was in fact there to read English.

A further awkward teenage reminder that I wasn't cut of the finest intellectual cloth came at a tutorial about Piers Plowman (oh come on, you must have read it). A Middle English classic, so a bit like Chaucer but with less boozing, no bare breasts or arses, and more earnestness. I had a few stumbling blocks; firstly, I couldn't translate most of it; secondly, I didn't understand much of what little I could translate; and thirdly I didn't really see much relevance of that small part of the comprehended part. I said as much to the tutor, - that I found it all a bit intellectually intense. He said, I recall the words, "But isn't that precisely what we're here for?'. 'I suppose so' I replied, each second seeming like a month of academic embarrassment, as my downwards-cast gaze found great fascination in what was in all likelihood a plainly patterned carpet. As soon as I could pile into Evelyn Waugh, George Eliot and George Orwell, where I could cover the literary criticism niceties having actually read the text in a recognisable language, and with various TV and film adaptations available, I did so. So, all in all, and surely without any doubt, the taxpayer certainly gained unquestionable value for money in funding me to partially understand a few books.

One of the unexpected oddities of pitching up at Oxford was that so many students there had barely if ever seen a Jew. The few of us that there are in the UK (one in 250, far too few to monopolise anything much though it's true we have totally dominated Jewish burial grounds around the M25 periphery) are hugely concentrated in about three North west London/Hertfordshire Boroughs and ditto but smaller numbers in Manchester. Leaving vast swathes of the nation largely empty of Jews. In addition, Jewish parents rarely send their children to boarding schools, and those who are privately educated tend to be in the day schools of north and central London. Conversely, my class group at school had been over 50 per cent Jewish. Strange as this may sound, boys known to go to church were seen as slightly unusual; we had maybe two in our class versus perhaps 10 who did some sort of synagogue attendance (though not me, after age 13). At university, by contrast, there were practicing Christians in number. The "surprise" – which I guess now may be called a micro-aggression, with the 'micro' somewhat apt in context - was that many of the guys seemed disproportionately fascinated by circumcision, as if this tiny skin snip done on newborn babies was like having a second head. Honestly, it makes you wonder what they did on quiet Sunday evenings in Oundle or Radley. As a footnote, the antiquated gowns we had to wear for tutorials and formal dinners did at least enable one's forked tail to be tucked away discreetly.

The most illustrious runner whose Oxford era coincided with mine was Richard Nerurkar. Given the outstanding success he later achieved (Olympian at both 10,000 and marathon where he placed 5th plus numerous high placings at world and European championships on track, road and cross country) it's worth mentioning that even at his own school he wasn't the best runner in his age group. Leading the endurance charge out of Bradford Grammar School was Andrew Leach who went up to Oxford one year prior to Nerurkar. And he did so as English schools' cross country senior champion, the best of the best. (Though for accuracy I should mention that in the early 1980s more youngsters left school at 16 and these included the prodigious talent of Jon Richards). Leach's running career went very much on the back burner post university, to such an extent that when at around age 50 he reemerged and, now based in North Hertfordshire, made unsurprisingly rapid progress towards the top of his age group, even the eminences gris at Athletics Weekly couldn't find any prior data on his running from the pre-internet era. It was in fact his son Matthew who was more prominent, representing GB on track and road whilst based in the USA employed in the world of Big Tech.

Unless the Bradford-Keighley area of West Yorkshire offers some freaky genetic gifts, then there must be some amazing sporting nurturing in the school. Two key supporters of the runners in the 1980s were a maths teacher, Mr Brock, and a French & Spanish teacher, Tony Kingham.

A slightly earlier Bradford Grammar alumnus was Mike Longthorn who won the junior National Cross Country. Whilst a school mate of the above pair was Adrian Moorhouse who won Olympic Gold at 100m breaststroke in 1988. From the next generation of alumni emerged the prodigious triathlon brothers of Alistair and Jonathan Brownlee, Olympic gold and bronze medallists respectively and if that isn't enough, we can now add Emile Cairess, currently the UK's second fastest ever and with a wondrous recent 4th place in the Paris Olympic Marathon.

And if the University didn't have enough fast guys, what was then Oxford Poly (now Oxford Brookes) had its own very classy duo in Clive Tulloh (son of running guru in many guises Bruce Tulloh) and Ian Manners. The latter eventually had his peak years with Highgate, whilst through the younger age groups he was outstanding as both a student and with Clevedon in Somerset and Avon. Tulloh, whose father coached Nerurkar through his senior career, gave up his full running commitment relatively young in the senior age group though his subsequent career brought prominence in a different walk of life.

Running wise, aside from the reasonably well-known Varsity matches against Cambridge and the National BUSA champs, there were a few inter-college races on cross country and track and even road. We also took part in a numerically small but wickedly competitive Reebok students cross country league which took in most of the more engaged athletic universities south of Leicestershire (but not the mighty Loughborough). I found it strange at the time that several of the leading runners placed more importance on a result against just one other university than against the entire student population of the UK, and also that some very strong runners either neglected or barely engaged with the general club structure outside the narrow world of the Dark Blues set up.

Amongst the Reebok league's leading lights in my first year was Geoff Wightman, then doing a law degree at Bristol and he went on to run for GB and England at the marathon and then to have a notable career in the sport in various leadership roles. Back then I suspect that if you told him that 35 years later he would be commentating within the stadium in Eugene, Oregon as his son Jake powered home to take gold in the World Championship 1500 metres he might have dismissed it as barely credible fiction. Speaking of barely credible fiction, one of the perhaps less vaunted strands of his CV may be his authorship of the novel Triathlon Armageddon. If nothing else (and as Geoff is a lawyer, I truly am not suggesting that there is nothing else) the novel puts to bed any notion that full on triathlon training has a deleterious effect on the male libido.

In a very bad piece of timing for which I've never truly forgiven my metatarsals, the first decent ongoing period of training I could do after I left school was just when I was close to finishing university, so frustratingly I was always on the outer margins of the university running – slow, sporadic and fleshy for about eight out of nine terms.

4

CLUBLAND, HOW WE GOT HERE

The club system continues to be the bedrock of depth in British distance running. This is not just lazy patriotic bluster, but a view which comes via numerous overseas runners. In London we have had numerous seasoned runners relocating from all of the leading European athletics nations and without exception they admire the number of clubs with high level runners aplenty. The best way to show this nationally is to scroll down the rankings at the endurance events. Whilst the sporting media will, at a stretch, pay some attention to the top handful, it's the sort of performance that only ranks you 37th or 93rd that is the real indicator of the merits of clubland. If you can compare to the likes of, say France, Italy, Germany, Poland and Spain, you'll see that the UK surpasses them by large margins.

There's no single or obvious explanation for this. Maybe the now vanishing heritage of the 1960s to 1980s has some subliminal legacy effect; maybe the series of national club team champs and the prestige they still hold amongst the inner circle of the leading 15 to 20 clubs still counts; and thus you bring together the combination of athletes, coaches, and team management to make these things happen. It remains almost entirely amateur in that the runners don't receive any fees for any results within this circuit of competition (though the leading lights will pick up bits and pieces elsewhere). And by and large most of the coaching is done on a voluntary basis (though this is an evolving aspect) and so is all the supporting work around the events, which exist almost in a separate competitive realm from the increasingly commercial mainstream of distance races.

If you want to find a weak link you could argue that at the top level just below world class the lack of funding means that runners increasingly tend to travel to the USA to try and facilitate the next step up, and that the crushingly narrow world class focus of the Lottery funding leaves a small but very talented pool of runners in a kind of no man's land where they work full time jobs and have to compete internationally against peer level runners with, one way or another, slightly more favourable funding options supporting them.

If you scroll through the list of all UK affiliated athletics and running clubs (don't say you haven't ever been tempted) you will see a hugely disproportionate number which were founded in 1981-82. They are very rarely called 'Harriers' or 'Athletics Club' but far more likely 'Runners', 'Running Club, 'occasionally 'joggers' or even 'trotters'. (Honourable mention here for Dorset Doddlers whose county location offers a nice alliterative name). This was of course almost wholly tied in with the first London Marathon in spring 1981, and in that and the following year almost all the main cities in the UK set up their own marathons. Many went by the wayside; some have continued ever since and others have had a start-stop-start history. The 'stop' years were invariably linked to the upwards trends in road traffic so that 'quiet Sunday mornings' became a thing of the past in terms of road usage and over this period the police started making a full charge for maintaining traffic free routes where required – hugely adding to the events' overheads. There was no significant drop in runners at any stage, just varying rates of growth in numbers of participants.

Certainly in the early years of these new breed clubs there was a very clear distinction between the old clubs and the new – the latter had only adult members, often predominantly veterans (40 plus; just don't get me started on the Veterans 35 category); they focused on long distance races and for many of this new era their running 'careers' started at the marathon, a total inversion of the usual endurance pathway, which ended up at the 26.2 miles after working through the other events. The new clubs often had their HQ at a pub, or a community centre (younger readers, ask your parents what these used to be) or even a car park. An old club would nearly always be based at the local track and big swaggering clubs like Shaftesbury even had bases at two tracks, Copthall in Barnet and a second group at Harrow; and the social side would generally be a far more prominent aspect of the new clubs' PR.

The cringey strapline of "A drinking club with a running problem" was frequently used although now looks rather dated because of its light-hearted sideways reference to alcoholism. A serious athletics club would never officially major on boozing as one of its recruitment tools. Though informally the post-session pub may be embedded in the club.

A good number of the front end members of the road running clubs had a 'shadow life' running in higher level races for the nearest Athletics Club, so on a Saturday afternoon you might get buried towards the back of 16 lean tight-jawed fellows in a national league 5000 metres in an intense track event for your AC and then pitch up on Sunday morning to win a low key 10k fun run, wondering what do with the unwanted bottle of Baileys Irish Cream that came with the winning trophy. Over the decades some shades of athletic grey emerged – with the decline in the total number of serious track and field athletes, many supposedly better ACs struggled to fill their squads across the less populated events, whilst some Running Clubs, if they had just a couple of athletes who could sprint and jump a bit, could start to cobble together a track team. And whilst the AC's tended to be fine up to 10k and Cross country and road relays, they had no great numbers at marathon, whilst the new clubs, partly by sheer weight of numbers and indeed some motivational camaraderie at the pub gatherings post run, produced some strong marathon squads.

And if you are good at marathon you are going to be at least solid at 5k and 10k and so the endurance spectrum was covered by some 'recreational' running clubs quite effectively. And as these runners aged, they would in the main have children and so the roots of Young Athletes sections were laid. (Though there is almost no pattern of any of the new clubs developing and, importantly, retaining high level young athletes;

the keenest and best invariably move to established athletics set ups). In around 2010 the knock-on effect of these new clubs becoming rather less new, and taking on some traits of the old athletics clubs, meant that a third strand of clubs evolved – those newer and, likely to be slower, runners who perceived (inaccurately in many cases – it's worth stressing that point, as so many running clubs are so accessible to newer slower runners and most give clear website guidance on the minimum standard required) that there was no place for them and so set up an even more informal next tier of clubs.

So far, most of these outfits have stayed relatively small. It's now not even a talking point when so many of the leading runners in the UK marathon champs held within the London race are not from the ancient Harrier clubs. Possibly the highest profile example of elite performance via a new breed club is embodied in Olympic Marathon runner, former holder of the world best for 50k and, amongst many long-distance highlights, former UK 10,000m Track champion Alyson Dixon whose senior career was spent with the excellently named Sunderland Strollers. One odd historical fact is that she won the UK 10,000m title with no opposition on the day – not one of the Federation's finest moments in event hosting. It alters the phrase "You can only beat who turns up on the day" from a cliché to a philosophical debate. Coincidentally, her fellow Geordie Marathon Olympian, Charlie Spedding, entitled his wonderful autobiography 'From Last to First', which her single race covered in all its requirements in just 32 minutes.

With the decline in numbers competing in athletics outside the longer endurance events, particularly in the adult senior group (20s and 30s) numerous clubs through the 1990s merged to pool resources. Particularly in and around London, this merger mania, as the tabloids didn't describe it, produced some successful yet wordily titled clubs such as (take a deep breath here) Woodford Green and Essex ladies; Victoria Park Harriers and Tower Hamlets; and the thriving but hard to trot out in a casual conversation Windsor Slough Eton and Hounslow. It's useful as a guide to East Berkshire geography but tends towards wordy.

Outside the South East there was some resentment at this, with running clubs such as Eye, Wem, Rye and Ely aggrieved that the metropolitan elites were arrogantly snaffling up all the letters, with provincial clubs having to make do with the meagre scraps left behind. It was just fortunate that the few letters left available happened to be the names of these three-lettered teams.

One trend amongst newer clubs is that so many use the strapline of being the "friendliest club " that those not opting for this bland and largely meaningless option risk being suspected as satanists. I've belonged to two of London's self-proclaimed friendliest clubs and whilst they served me and countless others just fine on the social side, I fear that anyone meeting me as their first point of contact, especially if it's raining in a month when it's dusk at four o'clock, might not necessarily be convinced.

In recent years – perhaps the Covid era was a key stage in this little niche of running's evolution – there has, particularly in the larger cities, been a flourishing of running 'groups' which seem to draw in a much younger, even less formally structured and competitive crew. I'll admit that at my age and stage, and indeed where I wish to position myself in the sport – given that I can't reasonably cover all the bases – I don't really engage with this new strand and will just hope that those who wish to stetch their aerobic envelope towards its limits are aware of the range of other options in clubland.

Taxing Club Kit

My favourite running item was the less than legendary Inland Revenue team vest. The real benefit for long distances was the nice fit and particularly the really lightweight technical mesh that it was made from. It was a tricolour of white, orange and green horizontal bands and indeed showed how colourful tax officers and inspectors really were if given the sartorial opportunity. At the time the Inland Revenue (the forerunner of today's HMRC) had some very good runners. By far the most outstanding was Bernie Ford, world class on track, road and cross country and indeed an Olympic marathoner. If the tax guys had been allowed to compete in standard club competition, they'd have been around top ten in the nation. And that's not just because all the runners who worked as self-employed builders or plumbers would suddenly choose not to show up. To be clear, I worked in the Revenue for several years; I didn't just randomly search out sporting garments across the array of government departments. At least based on my experience there, it was a very runner friendly environment with great flexibility on working hours and, with few exceptions, low stress levels from the work demands. Indeed the low stress seemed baked into the system. My first day was on 24th November 1986 and on Day Two we had an introductory Welcome from the Office's head, who had the vaguely Orwellian job title The Controller. He said that "We are just about starting to wind down for Christmas" which seemed a nicely premature induction of Yuletide given that December hadn't yet arrived.

The only time I had any individual club coaching was around 1990 whilst I was with Muswell Hill Runners, a couple of whose quicker guys did some shared training with a comparable trio of Highgate's marathoners. To illustrate the clubs' pecking order mentioned above, the fastest Muswell Hill trio would have had about a dozen of the then Highgate 'A' team ahead of them in road and cross-country races. They received training plans and advice from that club's prolific and incredibly long serving Jack Bayliss who had, at a very early age, moved from middle distance running into coaching in 1966. The main tweaks he made in my handwritten schedules were slightly reduced overall mileage (though like countless other distance runners down the decades, I would usually sneak in a few extra miles), slightly edgier long runs, and - I think the most valuable adjustment - what he called "stepping stones". These were alternate miles shifting from in my case about 5.20 per mile to about 6.30 per mile, building such runs from about 10 to 15 miles in a marathon build up. These sorts of sessions are now fairly standard and are called different things, such as 'Under and Overs'. If used for Marathon prep I'd say that physiologically they help finesse burning fat at higher paces. That's not their only benefit and nor is it the only type of session to achieve this benefit.

Jack was hugely in demand by many younger athletes who were in the Highgate fold so after a few months I thought it unfair to add to the demands on his time but he was certainly very supportive, positive and thoughtful about the training and responsive to feedback as and when.

My early days of club coaching were at London Heathside – by virtue of my later running years being with Muswell Hill Runners which, as a result of a merger with North London AC, became a rechristened club in the late 1990s. It was on paper a classic merger of the era – an old style AC with a new breed running club that drew from a very similar catchment.

Serpentine Scribblings

I joined Serpentine in 2008, purely as a coach after my own running had fully hit the buffers, and after seeing a bunch of their lively crew at a coaching seminar I organised. I knew that they had, at the time, a relatively young set of runners; that there was close to zero organised coaching in the club; that too many of them had started at the marathon far too early in their running development; and that, marathon mania notwithstanding, they were a very smart bunch.

Over the following decade or so the men's squad made fantastic progress in the context of a club previously best known for bringing the best post-race cakes to events and for being first in and last out of the pub. The biggest highlights as a team were several times winning the UK and England team championships held within the London marathon, bronze and silver team medals in the tough and prestigious southern cross country championships and silver medals in the equally loaded southern 12 stage road relay championships, a 4 hour mammoth event covering close to 50 miles. Also notable for a supposed marathon club was the team gold in the UK 10k Championships incorporated within the BUPA (now Vitality) race in London.

Whilst Nick Torry was the standout individual for several years, several of the big team gongs were won without his inclusion so the depth just behind him was excellent. If you look through the list of famous club names that the Serpie guys managed to beat, from a previous base as a recreational running and triathlon club, it was a superb few years with great team camaraderie. As a further illustration of the team's strength, one year the Welsh marathon championship was held within the London event and Serpentine man Richard Phillips won the Welsh title in 2 hours 23 minutes but finished outside the club's scoring team in the

UK race.

A handful of the chaps ran for England and Wales on road and cross country, capped by Nick Torry. A late starter in the sport, after a couple of, for him, initial recreational marathons, he sensibly put that distance on the back burner for a while, hacked into his 5k and 10k times before resuming duty at 26.2 miles. This led him to a 2.15 PB and an inspiring selection for Team England at the 2014 Commonwealth Games in Glasgow. It was thrilling to be on Clydeside to watch him justify his place on a typically drizzly and gusty Glasgow morning.

Nick shifted to the ever-strong Kent AC after the pandemic and keeps bashing out almost groundbreaking races to keep the years at bay. As his 47th birthday approached he placed 17th in the gruelling Southern cross country champs in the thick of guys running close to 30 minutes for 10k and then once into his 48th year he achieved a staggering 65.37 in winning outright the always strongly contested Paddock Wood half marathon and equalling the British record in the V45 category, and with a couple of extra years on the clock versus the man whose mark he equalled. That time has stood unbeaten for 40 years as evidence of its outlying quality. The following month he sped to another landmark performance – 2.18 at the London Marathon, just a minute slower than the UK best in the V45 group, and of course with him 'giving away' a couple of years to the younger standouts in the age group. Always a relatively quiet guy he doesn't broadcast any training "secrets " though he has been holistic and consistent in incorporating resistance/ strength and conditioning to support the running load and in times of injury has bitten the aerobic cross training bullet for as long as needed.

It is purely speculation but seeing how he progressed and the relatively late stage that it all happened, I think that if everything had happened five years earlier the 2.15 Commonwealth Games runner might instead have been a 2.10 Olympic athlete.

Another long-term Serpie standout who happens to be just slightly older than Nick and thus his own outlying veterans achievements fall just a slither behind Mr Torry's is Will Green whom I coached and subsequently "advised "for several years, as described in Chapter 8.

One particular Serpentine club officer provided some solid glue to this team framework. As a late starter in the sport, and some way short of the leading lights with a 3.09 marathon PB Tom Poynton truly understood the top end of club athletics. He was throughout the peak era a strong lobbyist for the big hitters, as the relevant committee rep, and carried out numerous behind the scenes admin tasks to ensure the guys had some of the Boring But Essential things efficiently taken care of. A career-long Whitehall civil servant Tom had learned the art of hedging one's communication bets so as not to be shown to be 'incorrect'. In the admittedly unlikely event of a Serpie ducking under the 2 hour marathon barrier one could imagine Tom starting a PR report "In what may well be one of the leading club performances in recent years....."

Any high achieving team is likely to have at least one, and likely more than one, larger than life charismatic character around whom people feel that extra bit of motivational oomph. It's not something that people learn or try to be; it's just how they are. So, observing from my perspective, Serpentine had the likes of Richard Phillips, Hugh Torry and Chris Wright as looming presences. Whilst results could never be guaranteed, the one thing that was assured was that you would never be bored with people like this around. The chaps were always humble about their performances and when race organisers offered free entries to those at the sharp end and they never omitted the speech marks when referring to their "elite" entries.

That above-mentioned Southern Cross-country race also hosted one of Nick's less revered moments as a leading Serpentine light around 2019. At a brutally tough Brighton course in wet and blustery conditions he arrived nice and early to collect his number and chip and to talk about fartlek and single leg glute bridges with his teammates. Over some 50-plus minutes up hill and down muddy Sussex Downs he ploughed through to about 17th, returned to his kit bag to get into dry clothes and out from the kit bag peered his racing chip. No chip meant no official performance, so he was not shown as a participant, rather rough justice given the immensely gruelling effort he'd just completed. Serpie strength on the day meant that the replacement scorer still secured team bronze medals. They rolled with the punches though gold would have glistened brighter.

From a performance perspective (and that was never intended to be Serpentine's key priority, it just happened, organically, to bring together the right people at the right time) the club took a big hit from around 2019. Covid didn't help but the pandemic was hardly a club-specific challenge. Any inner London club, in any sport I would guess, has an element of churn as people move to London in their 20s, very often from overseas and, in endurance running at least, often in high status jobs. Then typically around age 40-ish they may move out, with house prices a huge factor, as well as broader quality of life aspects which will be different as one's life evolves. At Serpentine the churn became only an exodus and in an approximate two-year spell about 80 per cent of the 'A team' had left. What goes around comes around so after 40-something years in the sport my coaching time at Serpentine had run its course after thirteen very lively and fulfilling years.

On To Highgate, Belatedly

I wanted to be in a club where aiming for high performance (that is, the best level that you can reach) was a given for the majority of active members, not an eccentric little strand. A detailed and, as I expected, enticing phone conversation with the inimitable Ben Pochee did the trick and so after geographically skirting around but never joining the club for over 40 years I somewhat belatedly pledged my coaching troth to Highgate Harriers. Suffice to say that at no point in those decades had the club missed out on my contribution, least of all as a runner. On the men's side they had hit a peak around 1990, held it for maybe 5 years and then, as I followed their fortunes from neighbouring local club London Heathside, things had rather waned and the fast guys in their late 20s had lost a bit of ground down the years but not been fully replaced by new blood.

No club can ever be a one person show but the timeline of the gradual rebuilding tallies very closely with when Ben Pochee started to put his unique style and ideas into this 'project'. He describes very succinctly his own trajectory through the sport.

"I joined the club in 1984 and found what turned out to be my lifelong Highgate tribe doing the Young Athlete League together and led by the inspirational youth club coach Rob Kenyon.

My proudest PBs were as a youngster, 4:25 for 1,500 metres steeplechase and 5:51 for 2,000 metres steeplechase, and these times won me National (AAA) silver and English Schools Championship Bronze. I represented England once for cross country aged 17 or 18 (Belgium), on the track I was picked for GB international U19 team (steeplechase in Greece) and was then told I was a day too old for the competition. Suffice to say I took my ire out upon my poor mum's inability to hold on for another 24 hours.

I went to Loughborough Uni 1989-1992 to study Sports Science and spent the majority of my three years learning about being seriously injured for the first time in my life. Throughout my 20s I was injured more than running, then aged 33 I snapped my Anterior Cruciate Ligament at a Watford British Milers Club meet as I landed in the water jump. The irony was that my steeplechase race was a last-minute decision to try going sub 9 minutes and I was only really at Watford to cheer on my mate Ben Noad who was competing in the 10,000m which had the British Champs integrated.... How life goes full circle.

I had ACL reconstructive surgery, and after 12 months got back to racing and then snapped my Tibialis Posterior racing a duathlon. I took a couple of years out to race road bicycles all over the UK and raced in Belgium where I experienced racing atmosphere nirvana and I did wonder why track racing didn't have this energy. 2009 I had Tib Post surgery, I spent 5 long months in a leg cast and eventually got back to running decently as a 40 year old, where I race the Bedford county 10,000m Championships (30:46) with a group of non-county athletes that were summoned together via a Facebook call to action, and hence was sewn the seed in my head of Night of the 10,000m PBs potential."

At around this time he also shifted toward team management and non-specific Maker of Great Stuff Happening. He is full of creativity, charisma and wit and he does all this devoid of ego and certainly not for monetary gain. His early years were spent right on the Highgate doorstep at William

Ellis school and as creative as Ben is, I think it's fair to say he hasn't yet matched the cultural legacy of fellow alumnus, the folk-rock legend Richard Thompson. Though I would bet against Mr T being able to seed a series of 10,000 metre races with the accuracy of Mr P.

The engaging oddity about Ben's unique Highgate presence and influence is that eight years ago Ben moved house. Of course, sorting out the Stamp Duty bill and making sure the Wi-Fi and gas supply transfer seamlessly, whilst also having to coax a bunch of intelligent adults to show up at the Metropolitan cross country league isn't exactly the most daunting bit of multi-tasking. But the Pochee relocation was deep into Cornwall, not even the nearest bit where Devon ends, and from where you can drive out of the county without needing a toilet stop en route. So for a club where the large majority of the regulars live within about four miles of Parliament Hill as the crow flies, this driving force fulfils his role at a distance of some 310 miles or just under 500 kilometres to make it sound even further. There's a case that once you are away from the immediate locale, it doesn't matter hugely whether the distance is 20 miles or 2000 miles, given the power, range and variety of modern communications, with the big caveat that it does require a deep previous foothold with the remote club you are working with.

Ben is an immense believer in the power of the collective and it so happens that the club endurance season at area and national level is based around numerous options to maximise the benefits of teamwork. There are the two early spring 12 stage relays, in which the four hours of racing time seems to pass very quickly, and the Metropolitan Cross Country League, which require 12 per team. I've assumed that this fixation on 12 is an old empirical measurement hangover. But whatever, 11 or 13 would seem peculiar in the circumstances. In addition, there are two early autumn 6 stage relays to mirror the 12 stages. I seem to be in a minority in thinking that if you had to create a national club season from zero you might not set up 4 road relays, given everything else that has to be fitted in. (Oh, three weeks after the national 6 stage relays with each leg about 6k, there is a national Cross country relay – teams of 4 each racing 5k. Different surface but – well, you get my drift…)

Ben is adept at being bang up to speed on modern comms when that matters, whilst drawing on old traditions when that can add to the vibe – so the club is big on the '1879' date of its foundation, one of the very oldest in the country, and it uses the basic logo of an old style farm gate as an easily identifiable visual icon. You can probably work out whether the gate is low or high. (Highgate was an outer London farming village until deep into the 19th century, decades before the Russian kleptocrats who have bought up some of the area's gated mansions had their money to launder. These vast abodes have great views from their upper levels of Parliament Hill's key cross country races – this is one of the underpinning factors in their outrageous prices.) Maybe it is something to do with age - Ben is now over 50 - as his team based motivational content is now at least as much about experience, memories and shared positive values as it is about the result itself. Although it's not in doubt that winning something is likely to help with the quality or depth of the experience.

One Highgate Harriers training trait I initially picked up decades ago was that the Sunday long run was done at very leisurely pace. I would occasionally bump into some of the crew - including Mr Pochee himself - on a Sunday morning and it was immediately noticeable that they were going slightly slower than I was. They were rather more accomplished racers and I was not particularly punchy, for my level, on longer runs. This pattern still persists so if you are minded to Strava some of the chaps' longer runs you will very often see something like 2 to 2.5 minutes per mile slower than their 10k race pace. They tend to chat away, often about what they've spotted on their own Strava "research". This is usually the day after a testing Saturday morning effort though.

Historically Highgate had seemed relatively low key and old school on the concept of individualised coaching and the majority of their success down the years was based on key group sessions twice weekly and plenty of easy and steady miles over the rest of the week. One heard relatively rarely that runner X was coached one-to-one by coach Y and I found this approach refreshing. The trend to ensure that supposed "unsung heroes " in coaching are given due recognition has arguably swung the other way in recent years so it's pleasing to see that many runners with a certain level of knowledge, experience and objectivity can make a very good job of plotting their own training and progression. Before joining the club

I checked with Ben that my impression was broadly accurate.

I'd also seen that the club was fairly light touch on marathon and most of the runners saw 5k and 10k as perfectly worthy goals in their own right rather than a staging post on the way up to the inevitable marathon. The general pattern with marathon specific training at higher level is that it can "take runners away" from some of the group structures. That is, long sturdy Sunday runs mean that Tuesday track sessions may be put on the back burner and similarly the club's Saturday morning threshold sessions don't neatly align with those long Sunday efforts. It's hardly a matter of conflict but it does slightly shift the club-based commonality of purpose in some cases for some of the time. Again, I warmed to this approach as it bucked the trend in so much of the distance running world, where it can seem as if everything is there to serve a marathon goal. That said, a few more of the club's quicker runners had done or were planning to do serious marathoning.

In another example of running life going full circle, my first year of Highgate coaching was done trackside with Jack Bayliss, thirty years after he had guided my running. He then had fifty -five years of continuous coaching experience – a longevity very rarely matched. Perhaps in line with the club's broadly 'light touch' coaching tendency beyond the two weekly group sessions, was just over a year before anyone at Highgate actually came forward for any individual coaching and advice. This timescale didn't worry me as almost everything about coaching is a long game.

Latecomer's 12-stage Ramblings

In early April whilst the majority of the modern running world is focused on marathons (indeed with the likes of London, Boston, Rotterdam, and Paris plus numerous other A listers it is arguably THE marathon month) the biggest concentration of high-level UK endurance runners, by some margin, pitches up in Sutton Park in Sutton Coldfield near Birmingham for the legendary national 12 stage. It's a mammoth event, runners alternating longer legs of 8.6k and 4.8k in the undulating West Midlands suburban park. The winning time is invariably a shade over four hours and the margins after such a length, just shy of 80 kilometres/50 miles, are always tight.

The event in its current format has been going almost 60 years and its leading teams give good insight into the nation's athletic history over these decades. Indeed, at a stretch they reflect economic and social trends. In the early years the locations of the winning teams show how lean young men used to make or indeed mine things in the West Midlands (Tipton, near Wolverhampton), the Northeast (Gateshead) and South Wales (Swansea). Indeed, in the first 25 years of the event just one single team medal (out of 75) was claimed by a club in London. One year the Tipton crew were so confident that as their 12th stage fellow crossed the line to secure team gold the squad immediately put on their pre-printed 12 stage champions T shirts. Hubris waiting to happen, but they got away with it.

More recently the balance of power has shifted towards the conurbations such as Leeds and London and the Southeast. To indicate the tremendous standard, to be in with a winning shot a club's six long stage runners need to be worth sub 31 for 10k at the worst, and then you need 6 shorter stage guys able to break 15 minutes for 5k. That is quite an ask for the 12th man in a single club set up. Typically, on the day there will be maybe 50 runners with some sort of international selection on their CV and a handful of pros, pitching in for their club for no monetary return.

The fastest ever longer stages show a Who's Who of UK endurance elite over the years. One weak leg in a leading team (in this context a slower than 16-minute 5k runner would be such) and the gap conceded is too much for any single big hitter to claw back.

Rather belatedly in my coaching days, the first time I came to this festival was when Peak Serpentine came in force off the back of silver medals in the southern event held two weeks prior. The guys placed an excellent 9th, quite likely the highest ever achieved by a new breed running club and great evidence that the club at the time was not just for marathoners.

Moving to Highgate, things ratcheted up a notch. Ben Pochee, increasingly supported by Rob Wilson, the Men's Team Captain and a tremendously able and popular man he is, has masterminded the spring focus and he stresses that on the day it offers 12 men the rare opportunity to emerge as national champions in athletics, something very few will ever be realistically able to achieve on an individual basis. The club won the race in 2016 and took silver in 2018. In the last three years the Men's A team has placed 2nd, 2nd (English Champions, behind race winners Central AC, from Stirling in Scotland) and 3rd – and each year the drama has continued right through the 12th leg. And to round out the club's team spirit and depth, the Highgate B team has placed around 20th. That might not sound especially notable but it's quite a feat to place that highly in the UK with a team that by definition has to omit its fastest 12 runners.

I'd guess that at least 95 per cent of active British runners don't know that this race even exists.

My Racing Moments in Club Days

It's only been in more recent years as a coach, both voluntary and otherwise, when I mix with a greater diversity of current and former runners than I ever did when I was 'just' a runner, that I have realised that compared to plenty of runners, I didn't actually love the running activity that much. Maybe paradoxically, there are those who run much less than I used to, and have less ambition on the performance side, for whom going running – that is, the movement itself - seems more essential; in the literal sense, being part of their essence – than it ever was for me. On the same principle, there are certainly former elites for whom running was a phase they went through, in some cases as their actual job, and which has in later years fallen off their activity radar.

One newer, very recreational runner, towards the slower end of all who I have coached, said of his relatively late (mid 40s) conversion to running, "If I didn't do this, I'm worried what would happen without it". Excess eating, boozing, sloth, disintegration of a daily order in their life – many runners have running as an underpinning check and balance to what might otherwise become chaos, or at least how they perceive chaos. They don't know for sure that this would be the upshot, but they don't take the risk of having to find out whether it would be – and so the habit becomes embedded.

Don't be mistaken, there were major aspects of my involvement in the sport that were compelling and, for some years, irreplaceable to me, but on a 10 or 11 runs per week basis it wasn't always a joyful activity. I liked races but didn't especially like marathons. My own sensation was that running 10k at say 5.15 to 5.20 per mile, and a half marathon at just a few ticks per mile slower, felt quite exhilarating, the balance of fatigue outweighed by the feeling that I was going a long way reasonably quickly. Remember, with no middle-distance prowess to speak of, 5.20 per mile felt quite quick to me, though any much quicker athletes will justifiably think I was deluding myself what 'fast' was. Marathons, well, by and large at 5.50/5.55 per mile that edge of pace never really kicked in, it all became quite painful and invariably slipped in the final few minutes to the less sexy side of 6 mins per mile.

Sometimes it all felt a bit misguided, wearing a club vest, with a race number, having done all the numerous tasks that a race requires from leaving one's front door to getting to the start line, and yet end up racing the final stages slower than 6 mins per mile. I believe these feelings of existential doubt (that is, in this context, the purpose of 'existing' as a supposedly competitive runner) are not uncommon in runners and observers. A favourite quote to rub in the need for perspective and realism comes from a clubmate of the 1980s who in the old Liverpool marathon was asked by a non-running work colleague how he had fared. "Ninth in 2.31' was what he divulged. 'Oh well, at least you finished' was the response. Cheesy as it may sound, the former UK Athletics strapline of 'From Fun to Fulfilment' always seems tremendously apt and succinct for running – if you aren't deriving some element of each, then you are perhaps better off doing something else.

Snippets from the road

The most scenic race I ever did in Britain was the underpromoted but truly spectacular Rhayader 20 miles in the Elan valley in central Wales. Starting in the small market town the course has around 3 early miles running up along the side of a mountain with the reservoir and countryside beneath you. The road is actually stretched out along a reasonably manageable gradient so it's not as gruelling or indeed as slow as "running up a mountain " sounds. At the crest there's an approximate 3 miles descent to match, again the gradient is not so severe as to bash the quads. The remaining two thirds of the course, with spectacular reservoir setting amidst the Cambrian mountains, was fast going albeit with a little climb in the final mile back into the town. The first year I went with a Shaftesbury crew and the fact that the course was clearly short by almost a mile compelled us to slightly numb the disappointment with an extended evening in the pub. The following year the race organisers added the extra distance, and I had a very pleasing run, placing 3rd and taking home a stash of the local crystal wares as reward. Today the race is established at 30k and is still an underpublicized jewel in the racing calendar where it slots in ideally for spring marathon prep. Highly recommended.

My first random brush with Seb Coe was lining up just behind him in about 1986 at a 4.9 miles (just don't ask why) league road race in Victoria Park, East London. The second thing I noticed - the first being "Jeez it really is Seb Coe" - is that whilst he only has three extra inches of height on me, his waist seemed to be in line with just below my neck. I thought what a rough deal life had dealt him, such a relatively short torso. He placed 4th (outsprinted, would you believe) behind Keith Penny, Ossie Arif and winner Steve Crabb. It's a shame really, as aficionados can never lose sight that whilst the two Olympic golds and sackload of world records are, superficially at least, impressive, the glaring lack of a Chingford League victory does tend to leap out from his CV.

The second occasion was sedentary and more illuminating, a coaches' workshop in a Guildford hotel organised and chaired by the outstanding and sadly now deceased coach Dave Sunderland. It was spring 2011 and given Seb was somewhat invested in London 2012 it was gracious of him to give his time purely for the benefit of the sport. What came across to me was how relaxed and unforced he was with no pressure to "perform ", no product to sell, no federation corruption or doping scandal to push back against; and, whilst he is not exactly short of ego, he knew that the audience knew exactly both what he had achieved as an athlete and a great deal of the journey to get there. So, as it were, there wasn't anything to add to that, nor any need, to

*impress us further, so it was just a bunch of coaches chewing the endurance fat.
I noticed he stayed seated for the duration, his torso dimensions cunningly
occluded.*

My very marginal personal dalliances with "professional " running in
my own mediocrity were as a result of placing 2nd and later 3rd in the
now defunct Slough marathon. In the first few years of paid athletics,
sums were initially paid into a trust fund held by the governing body
against which the athlete then claimed the sum to meet their associated
costs of training and racing. So it was with a vastly inflated sense of self-
importance that I did the necessary to draw down the £150 and £100
that Slough Borough Council had awarded. I was once outsprinted for
first place in a North London low key road race where the winner was
awarded the somewhat generous prize of a TV. Of course, one deals
swiftly and maturely with these minor setbacks and within two or three
years I could readily switch on my home TV without being twisted with
deep resentment that I'd had to buy the thing. And the Biro I earned for
2nd place had no end of regular use for shopping lists and training dairy
records. Though green ink wouldn't have been my preference.

The one marathon where I was in a race rather than a battle to simply
run as fast as I could for the distance, was in Harlow. It had formerly
been one of the leading UK marathons before the big city events
remodelled the events calendar. The fact that on a day of persistent
heavy rainfall a leading group of seven of us pootled through 22 miles in
2 hours 12, exactly 6 minutes per mile, albeit with rain-heavy feet, tells
you that the line-up was not exactly the national elite. Mentally it was an
interesting one off, knowing that the pace was going to pick up at a very
late stage, and not knowing how we would all fare when this happened.
The guy who took off and ran the final 4.2 miles at 5.30 per mile was
the older brother of someone who played over 300 matches as a Chelsea
midfielder so he'd gained the relatively short straw on the sporting career
option, with a winner's trophy and some swag from an Essex New Town.

Perhaps strangely the most satisfying marathon I did was some
minutes slower than my best. It turned out also to be the last one that
I was able to count, without being scuppered by the 'career ending' injury

mid race. I had torn a meniscus in a sharp turn in Finsbury Park in early 1993 and whilst the initial pain was severe it reduced somewhat but was nowhere near 'cured'. In summary I missed most of the next three years whilst the full detail of the tear was never truly diagnosed. In 1996 I had a double meniscectomy and took several months of gradual rehab. The advice from the surgeon and the physio (the late Neil Black, dumbing down to my level) was that because of the risk of osteoarthritis in the operated-on area I might consider restricting my training and racing to a maximum of half marathon. For about 18 months I did so, so former 85/90 miles weeks became 55-60 miles and I was a few per cent slower. At the least injury-bothered phase I had one last push for the marathon in 1999, in London, and cobbled together a training block of around 60-65 miles average per week plus an hour or two on a cross-trainer bike. It had been a 6-year gap since my last marathon so – far more than for any previous marathon – I was just delighted and relieved to even be on the start line. I made it round in a pleasing – in the context – 2.38 and then followed about 3-4 years of further meniscus deterioration and the non-negotiable evidence of osteoarthritis in the left knee.

By far the most frustrating race I ever finished was the Poly Marathon – a former classic race (indeed it had hosted a few world best times in the 1950s and 1960s) in West London that had fallen away as the build-up of suburban traffic did its worst. It was restored for one year in around 1992 and I was in my best shape for the distance. Finally, I felt able to maintain an even pace for the full distance. And so it was proving; with former world class runner Hugh Jones way ahead in the very late stages of his pro career, I was pottering along nicely sharing third place with a runner who, I learned, worked as a fireman in Liverpool. That's the nice thing about running at optimum marathon pace; you can hold a decent conversation for at least the first half. So, I'd found out about his family, domestic pets and work rota and in return I'd regaled him with a favourite Ken Dodd gag - "Oh in Paris they're so sophisticated; they put out tables and eat their meals on the street. In Liverpool we call that eviction". We were still running even splits, right on course for 2.30 or 2.31 at worst, when at mile 22 somewhere around the Richmond vineyards the two of us missed a marshal and went astray. After a mile or so we realised that the total lack of race markers or further marshals probably meant what we crushingly thought it meant, and so we retraced our steps. I referred above to the last stages of a 26.2 mile marathon being 'quite painful'. I'd use slightly different words to describe the last 2 miles of this 28.2 mile excursion but will leave them unwritten.

As a much younger runner I had always been convinced that 'serious' running past 40 wouldn't interest me – I trained very hard for numerous years when at my physical peak and it made no sense to me to intend to do the same to just get slower and slower in doing so. I had set a baseline of 2.45 marathon as being the slowest that would make sense to me, and for me, to do. I had some vague idea that once I couldn't achieve this I would just trot around running a daily hour or so for all the things that were enjoyable about the activity outside the racing bit. It didn't really affect me to the core in the way you might expect. As it happened, the knee took away the options and gradually – so gradually that almost no one beyond me noticed it month by month - the running seeped away. I think about the last run I ever did was at about age 51 and by then it had been clear for at least three years that it was just a matter of time.

Cheshire Elite Marathon 2021 – One Off Inspiration

One of the most inspiring events of the covid era - indeed one of the most memorable club events I've been at over the decades - was the Cheshire event which involved a huge amount of planning and replanning as the health and government regulatory landscape evolved over the pandemic. The back story was that the race director who operated in the Cheshire and Welsh border area wished to satisfy the racing demands of the UK championship runners who would normally have their big domestic target in the London marathon in late April.

He made clear that the entry standards would broadly mirror those of the London championship and settled on 2.40 for men and 3.00 for women which would thus likely throw up about 400 entries from the UK and, as things excitingly transpired, abroad. An extra spice was added when, with the Tokyo Olympics deferred from 2020 to late summer 2021, the April race date offered a potentially tailor-made opportunity to achieve the qualifying time. The race organiser had numerous local authority and governing body hoops to go through, all exacerbated by the pandemic, and given the niche entry standard he was clearly motivated only by the runners' hopes rather than any possible financial return.

The course was as near ideal as could be, just under four very flat laps on the Cheshire border with Wales through lovely rural lanes with some shelter provided by trees along the route. From a coaching perspective I was hugely excited by this one-off as there had been something close to a racing drought for a full year, and almost all coachees within the qualifying time had this as a target.

The weather behaved itself and the event delivered all that could be asked, and indeed more. The lead designated pacemaker, enigmatic British youngster Jake Smith, did his role to the letter, metronomically clocking 5.00 per mile until deep into the race. Still not quite spent, he bypassed the usual pacing role which entails stopping, and raced home in 2.11.00 as the overall winner in his unplanned debut. Even more, he shaved under the Olympic Qualifying Time albeit the UK trio had already been selected with slightly faster times so there was no controversy on that score. Second place was another debutant, New Zealander Callan Moody running for Serpentine, with a superb 2.11.38 falling just eight seconds outside the Tokyo Qualifying Time. Behind them the depth of mainly UK runners was tremendous, almost fifty men under 2.30 and given the small numerical scale of the event was even more memorable. Similar fireworks were lit by the leading women with several from overseas making this unusual trip in search of Olympic opportunities. Such that the five leading finishers fell between 2.28 and 2.31 and secured Olympic/ 2022 World Championships times for the likes of Ireland, GB and Israel. Personally, I'd enjoy this sort of event annually though with the usual roster of city marathons returning from autumn 2021 this wasn't really feasible.

5

KENYA – TEA, TOASTED TOAST
AND TEN THOUSANDS

The trip to Kericho in 2001 was something that I thought that as a serious runner I must do once to experience the world's most successful hub of endurance running. This was relatively early in the cycle of non-elite runners going to the Rift valley to train and it was an eye-opening fortnight. Perhaps it is the only nation on earth where its distance runners have such a role in representing its reputation to the rest of the world. Which is a good thing of course. But it does have a context.

Firstly, people are poor in the villages. There is indeed loads of sun, the scenery is varied and beautiful, with relatively little rain, no famine and a lot of smiles to be seen but the rural quality of life for most at least in 2001 was not great. Data on Kenyan income levels does not suggest any major uplift since. Male life expectancy is just 58 for men (though 63 for women) and the death rate in motor accidents is around 40 times that in the UK and most of Europe. I wrote this section in the week of the tragically premature death of 2.00 marathon world record holder Kelvin Kiptum aged just 24.

Food is very basic and whilst it's undeniably healthy and ideal for runners it is fairly drab and repetitive. Meat portions are scanty and not usually available daily on grounds of cost. This is fine for a travelling experience but imagine this for a lifetime. One oddity, again arising from the circumstances, is that Kenyan runners eat notably little solid food given their high energy requirements.

A vast amount of their calorific intake, I'd estimate at least a third, is made up through their tea, or chai, which is basically tea (a home-grown staple of course) made with heated full cream milk and drunk with high amounts of sugar. So if as a visitor you don't consume this beverage to fuel your training you will likely be arranging surreptitious trips to the chocolate and biscuit section of the local garage store.

A training quirk that I've never really understood is why the typical training slots are at 6am and 10.30, which seem embedded in their running culture. The early slot is not that unusual and, because it is near the equator it means that year-round this is around sunrise so you will invariably meet in darkness and finish in broad daylight. The second run is often a structured session at or from a track. This can give a strange time management scenario along the following lines. You finish the early run at around 7am. You heat up water to shower or at least wash, a slower process than in the west with our boilers, then you do likewise to heat up water for tea and heat some bread to eat toasted. (Kenyans describe sliced bread as toast even when it's not actually toasted so there are some odd little dialogues about non toasted toast). Then you eat breakfast. This may all take until about 8.30. If you have to drive to the next training session and sort out your kit, you may thus be left with just over an hour between the final part of concluding Run One and heading out for Run Two. The supposed explanation is that this leaves longer to recover between the second run of one day and the first run of the next, but it seems more of a cultural habit than a scientific path to optimal recovery. It does seem to work though and during my time no one seemed to find it a burden to their daily pattern.

This means that for each pro runner on a typical double day they will have numerous hours of relative downtime between wrapping up the second session and going to bed. How they spend these hours will vary immensely (albeit it will almost always be very light on physical activity) and arguably this will influence what they make of their lives once their running careers are over. If you are in two minds about trying the Kenyan running experience, then I'd say go with the mind that inclines to checking flight schedules to Nairobi. One unexpected trend was that several of the Kenyans, correctly assessing that this stumpy guy with early lines of greying hair was not likely to be at the cutting edge of Team GB's endurance squad, assumed I was an agent and were desperate to gain their first trip outside Kenya to make some money – and somehow word had got round that a 13.40 5000 (at altitude, remember) on their CV was the sort of level that could secure them a return airline ticket to somewhere with a handy prize list. So they all used this 13.40 benchmark to start the sweet talking. No doubt with the world depth having moved on the 'qualifying' time doing the rounds is somewhat faster. For those with some prior knowledge of the Kenyans' endurance prowess and running culture, a highly recommended book to tease out wider insights is Toby Tanser's 'More Fire' which spans a range of social and cultural insights; numerous fleshed out individual profiles; and plenty of training detail, by an author steeped in the sharper end of the sport for many years..

After the trip to Kericho I became one of a group of five runners who pooled some funds to set up a joint Anglo Kenyan training camp in the town and become just about the first European project to do so. We pitched in around £20,000 in roughly equal shares. This was almost entirely allocated to buy the plot and build the camp building itself which all happened relatively smoothly in around 2003/04. The Kenyan link was with one particular Kenyan elite whom we all knew and trusted. That trust proved to be our financial downfall. The athlete was one of the fairly early trailblazers in picking up numerous prize wins in UK road races. He was a bright man, raised as a farmer and very knowledgeable about arable and livestock and also machinery and some industrial aspects. Plus he managed his own racing plans very cannily and as he approached and indeed passed 40 years of age he turned to pacing roles to keep the racing income on the go. He spoke very good English and was a well-liked character. So the plan was that he would be the salaried on-site camp manager. The business model was based on a nominal (by UK standards) rent charge for Kenyan runners and a higher level for European runners which was both a modest sum from a European perspective whilst also offering a reasonable profit margin. In theory we had budgeted and planned for cooking, cleaning, massage, and training support.

Looks great, you must be thinking. We set up a standard but robust partnership agreement and included the clause that the land and buildings were held by the partnership. We had the land conveyed in the athlete's name, not in general a strange ploy given the aforementioned agreement and in this particular case we anticipated that having land ownership in the names of British muzungus would have led to massive profiteering by all those engaged in the subsequent building. In brief, the camp was never managed for the intended use, but instead was very quickly taken over by the athlete's family and extended family as part of their residential network. Revenue for the training camp has been zero, as has been the communication from the athlete to the people who funded the family's new abode. The reason we have never taken legal action to seek return of our lost funds is of course practicality and costs. The legal fees would no doubt eat up a large chunk of the misappropriated sum and there would need to be a couple of return trips to Kenya to establish exactly what has happened on the ground. As things stand, almost 20 years later, it seems that the athlete took a calculated gamble and thought he might well get away with it. As has been the case and not surprisingly, having this experience has rather influenced my assessment of the level of corruption endemic in Kenya. It is, you might think, of a piece with the worryingly high number of Kenyan runners caught doping.

I had had some other more favourable dealings with various Kenyans at various marathons over the mid-2000s. My friend, a coach who was the above-mentioned runner's manager, had become manager for a stable of 2nd tier Kenyans and Ethiopians. The standard set up was that in return for setting up their race entry deals plus travel and accommodation to races and in several cases, some coaching input, he received 15 per cent of their prize money and appearance fees (the latter were usually modest, rarely exceeding $2000.) He was adept at seeking out second level marathons in slightly off the mainstream places (Pyongyang in North Korea was one such though notably he didn't return there after the one visit. He did return to the UK though). On occasion he would "double book" with his athletes spread over two races and so I covered a few such races. These included Seville, Berlin, and Lahore. I felt uncomfortable being part of the commission approach, deriving more or less income from an athlete's performance on the day, so instead just asked for a nominal fee for my time away. And of course, whilst I had to take professional responsibility for the athletes whilst I was covering the role, it was a fascinating and exciting opportunity.

Not surprisingly the variety of athletes brought a variety of characters. Some larger-than-life role models, dynamic and out reaching in terms of learning languages and skills for their post running days and some much milder characters. The highs were seeing some relatively big wins for apparently fine honest runners, grossing maybe $20,000 which with the buying power in Kenyan rural areas at least 10 times the UK equivalent was a life changing sum. It was a joy to be around to see these moments; and I would be in the lead van so would see the front of the race unfold right in front of me. In general, these athletes were at a level where at the time $20k would be an unusual sum to win. There was a management skill to coordinating the "package " of a running team to a race organiser in particular for marathons where there is greater unpredictability. If you send four or five suitable athletes you have better odds that at least two will really shine on the day so this satisfies both the race organiser for the outlay on this little team and the manager who has at least two earners whilst one or two may have had poor runs. Sending just one runner has more likelihood to give a nil return. Bear in mind that it will nearly always cost well over $1000 to fly an athlete from East Africa to any international race because the whole Visa process means that tickets will never be booked much in advance and so the cheap headline fares will never be available.

I always found the whole professional African runner system both fascinating, exciting and repellent at the same time. Certainly, some of the overseas managers seemed extremely shady characters, fat heavy smoking men from ex Soviet nations with minimal experience in the sport, no empathy with the East African running culture but happy to seek out channels to carve out their 15%. Notably they were often from nations where a sum such as $500 went very much further than in the UK. So perhaps unsurprisingly the athletes were always on their guard against being ripped off by chancers and it's likely that the Empire history of Kenya compounded this (Ethiopia is a notable African rarity in having never been colonised by any of the European powers. Liberia is the only other always-independent nation in Africa – for anyone prepping for Mastermind whilst reading this). Conversely the managers were worried about naive or simply unscrupulous runners turning up at races in poor fitness, wasting perhaps $2000 of a race organiser's travel and accommodation budget. An unknown Kenyan dropping out of a marathon after 19k on the streets of a Spanish or Italian city hardly adds anything to the race's profile.

On one trip I had to sit for dinner at a table for two where the second place was taken by one of the earliest of a multitude of Moroccan runners banned for doping once the tests for EPO detection were introduced. Asmae Leghazoui had made a major breakthrough around 2001 and capitalised on this with some lucrative road wins across the distances below the marathon. She was strongly suspected and the combination of her small stature and the doping ban earned her the unenviable nickname on letsrun, then emerging as the world's leading internet forum for the endurance side of the sport, of Poison Dwarf. The 10k race in question where we broke bread was her first race back after serving her ban of just 2 years. She spoke enough English to comprehend what I would have liked to say, something along the lines of "What the hell did you think you were doing, trashing the sport just to earn more than you are worth? " That would have been rather an awkward ice breaker, so I just kept it banal and asked her if she had been training well. At another race a trio of Russian women featured prominently amongst the leading places and at the post race reception I asked one of them who their manager was as they seemed to have travelled unaccompanied to the race. A familiar name was mentioned; given what we know about how Russia conducts itself in sport this struck me as an appropriate linkage.

One race (not any of those mentioned above) had a rather troubling experience with the pro runner recruitment one year. I had been there the two previous years and there was a trend that the prizes by African standards were relatively generous for the times being clocked in the marathon and half marathon run simultaneously. The following year the sponsorship was bumped up substantially and similarly the prizes were ramped up about fourfold. It seemed that some managers saw the prize details which they set against the previous year's leading times and forgot to factor in that the goalposts had been moved with so many faster runners drawn in for the much larger prizes. The race organisation compounded the unhelpful scenario by flying in around 100 runners from East Africa whose number was boosted by some Russians and Europeans. This meant that with prizes being paid down to 10th man and 10th woman, inevitably dozens of professional runners would have a payless day, which in the marathon is not a sustainable career path. The prize money was (brutally, in my view) heavily front loaded so whilst a handful could wax fat once the dollars were paid, the 9th and 10th places would receive much lesser sums.

This produced a somewhat fraught evening after the race. Two runners came to my room, having earned precisely nothing, and described how on the planned sums they had anticipated from this race, they had borrowed from local villagers to pay for their younger siblings' education (state education in Kenya ends at age 14). They didn't spell out what would happen if they didn't honour the debt but I gathered it might be more forceful than a quiet chat over a cup of tea. Then there was a kind of financial mutiny. A Kenyan woman had been signed to pace the marathon to 25k, at a fee of $2500, which she had done excellently. Stil feeling full of running at her supposed drop out point she had pushed through to the finish, placed highly and earned a further $6000 by doing so. She argued that as the manager had only arranged her pacemaker role his fee should come only from the $2500 but not the added $6000. I said this was wrong and that she was only even in the race and able to carry on past the 25k mark because the manager's efforts had brought her there in the first place. I was convinced my view was correct but then had to run through this again when about six of her squad jumped in to her support. Perhaps it was no coincidence that this was the last time I covered this particular role.

One of the most extraordinary runner progressions I briefly witnessed in Kericho served to bolster my opinion that at some yet to be fully identified environmental level runners raised at this sort of altitude and, perhaps also relevant, descended from generations of altitude people, have advantages in this niche but very simple sport. A 17-year-old runner in around November 2000 had placed 7th in his local area cross country race for under 20s. Like a local authority area in UK, in terms of its scale within the nation, albeit with an incomparably higher number of keen runners

Then in January he had placed similarly in the area champs, so something like a UK county area. Then during my visit, we saw him place 5th in the Kenyan national cross-country champs at Ngong Racecourse near Nairobi, one of the sport's most astonishing spectacles. This secured him a spot in the Kenyan team for the world under 20 championship a month later. He placed 4th there too, with the top 15 places monopolized by East Africans as usual. So in 5 months he had progressed from a local level "one to watch" to almost the best under 20 on the planet and, I would estimate, a level that age for age no sea level runner has ever come close to matching. And there's more. In 2003 I watched on TV as this prodigious athlete ran on the track a dazzling time for 10,000m which still, over 20 years later, sits well within the top 10 of all time. He was not yet 20 when he ran this stellar 10,000.

Through this African management link there would occasionally be Kenyan athletes staying briefly at my home in Crouch End as they transitioned between the airport and the next race if it was in or near London. The weather always seemed to be wet, chilly and windy as if to remind them how different life here was from the Kenyan uplands. It was not uncommon for the runners to sit and quietly read The Bible which is a rare sight in 20th century London. Crouch End, about 3 miles from Islington, was and is very much a stronghold of Labour for whom spokesman Alistair Campbell had during that era famously pronounced "We Don't Do God ".

The Cabbage Patch 10 miles in October was a favourite for them, and whilst the famed Twickenham race is renowned for the large cabbages it gives its prize winners the top three were also given cash prizes that were more lucrative than any autumnal vegetable. Amongst the guests at the sea level abode were Joseph Riri shortly after a life changing mid 2.06 win at the Rotterdam marathon, then barely 90 seconds shy of the world record; and Patrick Macau. He was on his first trip outside Kenya as a late addition to the national team en route to the world half marathon champs. Later under a different manager he would briefly hold the world record with 2.03.38, one of the least well known of the World Record runners. He was the only Kenyan who downed more than 2 beers from the fridge. Ever the entrepreneur, he eyed my then four-year-old daughter's toy collection, mentioned his younger sister had a much smaller array and could he please take her home a small wooden horse. Fair enough.

6

PRACTICING SPANISH/SPANISH PRACTICES

Through a friend of a friend, I had the good luck to go to the Barcelona Olympics in 1992 and bypass both hotel costs and ticket scalpers by staying on this contact's city centre sofa and having him sort me a batch of athletics tickets through his Barcelona residency at the time. For the nation, this event (The Games; not my Catalan couch surfing, which received no media attention whatsoever. Given that the following month I placed 2nd in the prestigious Slough marathon I rather think they missed a trick there) was perhaps even more resonating than for other host cities as it came 16 years after the death of fascist dictator Francisco Franco liberated the country after almost 40 years of autocracy. Particular highlights were the eruption in the stadium as Spanish middle distance star Fermin Cacho stormed through to 1500 metres gold with a stupendously fast and tactically astute last lap; and GB golds for Sally Gunnell at 400 metres hurdles and Linford Christie at 100 metres.

Denmark in Catalunya

The one ticket I bought at an inflated price from a tout in Barcelona was for the session which included the men's 5000 metres final and, on paper, just about a medal shot for UK lead Rob Denmark. He had a tremendous change of pace and in 1992 was just before the big global long distance medals on the track became almost totally dominated by East Africans. The trend occurred about 20 years later in the women's events. In the event Denmark didn't quite have it on the day and the final wonderfully fast 200 metres went in the favour of Germany's Dieter Baumann. His last half lap was precisely 25 seconds and included having to chop stride and move out a lane. Baumann later served a strange doping ban, strange in that it was at the time arguably the most fervently and long contested ban that an athlete has put themself through. And of course, at immense emotional and financial cost. Baumann, who was always known as an intelligent and meticulously thorough character, pursued every feasible avenue to overturn the ban, even offering a narrative in which his toothpaste was sabotaged. Post ban, which stood as imposed, he basically returned promptly to his best levels and moved up the distances.

In later years I met Rob, who was also Commonwealth champion and European silver medallist at his preferred 5000 metres event, numerous times at an athletics centre which formed for both of us "our office " in our respective jobs at the time, his within UK athletics, mine in sports development. He was very lively and down to earth and graciously treated me as a peer within the sport once I'd banged on enough about watching his races to gain some credibility. I could have offered that memorable line from Stephen King's 'Misery' "Oh yes, I'm your biggest fan" though given how that plot proceeds to a somewhat gruesome denouement it was sensible to steer an alternative conversational path.

He was employed as an Athlete Services Manager by UKA to support elites and upcoming elites across events. He was at the time totally clear about having no coaching aspirations, as I asked him. So of course, he ended up moving into and upwards on the coaching pathway until he became a full time UKA endurance coach.

Out on the scenic Barcelona roads, long distance devotees could enjoy two gruesomely tough marathons which, as well as having the August warmth and humidity to battle against, obliged the runners to climb the savage Montjuic hills in the very final kilometres. Followers of the sport noted that the medalists never again truly matched the levels they achieved in this brutal race and the theory is that they pushed themselves just beyond the level from which they could fully recover.

This visit triggered my deeper interest in Spanish culture and of course Spanish running. I acknowledge that with the entire history of Spanishness on offer it took something as shallow as a few running races to press the button for me, but one has to start somewhere.

From the outset of Spain's sporting resurgence, which very roughly coincided with the awarding of Barcelona's host status in the mid-1980s, and the nation gradually being assimilated within the mainstream of democratic western Europe (it is one of the EU's most fervent and committed supporters) there were rumours of doping and particularly in endurance sports. Professional road cycling was a major sport across the nation, and that sport was essentially only doable at elite level with doping support.

Spain did however have various bona fide advantages in top level distance running, whatever pharmaceutical chicanery some may have succumbed to. It still had a large rural and small-town population with many people working at agricultural or manufacturing jobs and at this stage it had much lower obesity levels than the UK, plus in general a more natural and less processed diet. Also the Franco decades had left Spain largely devoid of the developed amateur harrier ethos and culture of the UK, so that when professional running opportunities emerged globally from the early to mid-1980s they were arguably less hide bound to old traditions. Spain also has numerous altitude training options with the Sierra Nevada high performance centre set stunningly in the mountains in the far South and a less cutting edge but centrally based hub in Navacerrada near Madrid (where Europe's highest yet straight and flat road is located, almost as if the landscape was designed for elite runners' needs) so this was certainly a contributor. The relatively low incomes in Spain meant that

a top flight runner had a better chance to live off his or her running than did a UK or German rival. Coupled with this the Spanish Federation via its national Olympic funding sources had a strong system of grants or becas. In addition, with Spanish people feeling a big sense of belonging to their local community, top athletes in Olympic sports could be awarded maybe a high four figure sum per annum by their local council in return for which they would provide some sort of coaching to youngsters or stadium/track management to fit conveniently round their training. In short there were far more professional adult runners in Spain than in the UK and the nation endured a golden era, particularly from the men's side from the late 1980s to the early 2000s.

Whilst British fans of a certain age may know the iconic photo of Sebastian Coe celebrating his second Olympic 1500 metres gold in Los Angeles 1984 , the most powerful image of Spanish Marathon pomp was that of the "triplete" who swept all 3 medals in the European marathon championship 1994 (the aforementioned Richard Nerurkar chased them home in 4th).

It is perhaps not entirely coincidental that the Spanish peak years were when EPO usage was at its refined peak for those who wished to partake but just before EPO testing was introduced in 2001.

I had a brief but, from my perspective, disarming conversation with one English-speaking elite who in the Noughties of the 2000s was on the possible fringes of Olympic selection given a bit of progression and a fair wind. He was living and breathing and thriving in an elite Spanish environment based mainly at moderate but helpful altitude. He had only positive feedback for some months. Then there was a brief training camp shortly before the track season started to which, against the trend, he was not invited. A week or so later the athletes returned, and this runner was startled to notice that several in the group were running harder interval sessions about 1.5 seconds faster per 400 metres, about 3 per cent, than the level just prior to the camp. His faith in the system almost instantly unraveled and he left the set up. A few months later I spoke to him, and he estimated that at the time about 25 per cent of the endurance elite were doping. This is of course doubly painful for the sport because inevitably it casts doubt on the hypothetical 75 per cent who are competing cleanly.

Through a bit of lucky networking via the great inspirational Birmingham coach Bud Baldaro, who had picked up on my Spanish enthusiasm, I acted as "Team Manager" for the single person team of Dan Robinson as part of his build up for the 2004 Athens Olympic marathon. Dan wanted a race of longish distance, warm weather and high depth at the front end and with nothing really on offer in the

UK in the required time window, I arranged a guest entry for him in the Spanish half marathon championship held that year in the remote Galician fishing town of Ribadavia. There were far worse ways to spend a summer weekend. Dan placed only a few places higher in the Spanish race than in the Olympics, so excellent was his Athens run. The following December I repeated the scenario, where off the back of his Athens result, he was provided with a trip to the Seville-Los Palacios Half Marathon and I was able to do the 'Team Manager' stint which was an exciting way to escape the London mid-December hassle for a weekend.

Dan had come late to the sport with no running heritage or previous hint of talent and initially started in his mid to late 20s purely to add some basic fitness for his Sunday league football. He used a treadmill at a local gym and at an early stage the duty manager noted the pace that this apparent newbie was sustaining and suggested he might usefully try an official event. As happens with the talented, he made very rapid progress, and an initial 2.37 marathon was really just a score on the door. A year later this was 2.19 and then the 2004 London brought the major breakthrough. The combination of a relatively accessible qualifying standard of 2.14 (relatively, in that this would soon evolve to 2.11.30, quite a chunk at this exalted level; and indeed to a spectacular 2.08.10 for Paris 2024 – a far greater advance than 'just' the advantages of the new shoes) and a dearth of UK runners at this level meant that his 2.13.53 as second Brit in the official Olympic trial secured his place at the iconic Athens Olympic event that summer. Arguably the hot weather and famously hilly course levelled the field slightly to the detriment of the fast track and half marathoners and in favour of those prepared to play a waiting game. In the event he placed 23rd, dozens of places ahead of where his PB ranked him. Always a pure marathoner and with relatively light racing history at shorter distances, he had an excellent 5-year spell including 2 world championships, excelling with 11th and 12th places, the Beijing Olympics and an outstanding bronze medal at the 2006 Commonwealth Games. As a lifelong cricket fan, he described his joy at entering the Melbourne cricket ground for the final lap of the track with third place secure.

He was very open and appreciative about his debt to his wife in enabling him to keep the voluminous training going through his peak years. Based in the Cotswolds and with, at the time one and then two infants, her full-time work in local government kept the family supported whilst he did part time PE teaching at a local school. His performance level was never going to attract significant lottery funding and without the truly momentous PBs he was not in a position to support himself just by his racing results. It's questionable whether, just 15 years later, this sort of narrative would be replicable given how marathon qualifying standards have been tightened.

The number of Spanish runners (including a number who immigrated from Morocco) who have served doping bans is not an admirable record and, whilst the nuances of the media's and Federation's coverage has shifted in recent years, they had a period when it was often reported in a slightly shoulder shrugging way. One conversation with a Spanish friend at the time epitomized the national attitude to corruption. He was an academic in the economics of sports venues and indeed had spent time as a postgraduate at a British University and was still enmeshed in the sport. We discussed the doping ban of their multiple national and European indoor record holder and champion Alberto Garcia which came as no surprise. I was struck by the way he offered up explanations which if not excuses seemed to me overly conciliatory. He spoke of the temptation of money, of the heightened expectations from the sporting public and the pressure of chasing the very rare (at that time) sub 13 minute 5000m. All of which were likely part of Garcia's mindset but not cheating should have sat in his mindset too, above these other factors.

Through this Madrid-based connection I had some dialogues with one of the Federation's leading coaching lights, Dionisio Alonso, who co-authored and edited the extremely thorough and educative book Great Moments in Spanish Marathoning. At the time he was coaching European indoor champion and 5000 metres specialist Jesus Espana. This is quite a portentous name and the athlete told how every time he checked in to big meetings outside Spain he had an extended process. "Name? "" Espana" "No, no not the name of your country, your name?" " Yes, that is my name and also my country". "Ok, and your first name?" "Jesus ". He had probably learned how to say, " Are you taking the pee, matey?" in all the main European languages. In a cartoon strip he'd have gone head-to-head with a stout-hearted Brit named Saviour Britannicus to even out the name game, though in fact in the 2006 European championship 5000m he just overcame by the proverbial chest (0.08 seconds) Mohammed Farah of Great Britain and Northern Ireland.

Another favourite Spanish endurance running and coaching book is 'Correr de otro modo' (Running Otherwise) by Antonio Serrano, the first Spanish runner to break 2.10 at the marathon and who has become perhaps the nation's leading endurance coach since moving into that role. I'll mention that I have every faith that these two coaches have always operated within the sport's rules. From a coaching perspective, the Federation every year published forensic papers from its high-performance coaching conference "Cuadernos d'atletismo" ('Athletics notebooks') where the minutiae of an athlete's long term training and development, or a detailed granular examination of a particular theme, would be set out across chapters of around 12 to 15 detailed pages. Fascinating and informative stuff.

One odd little remnant of Spanish Christianity, at least in the elder generations is that it can provide an eye-opening quote in running contexts. So when a Spanish 10,000m runner won the European Cup race in brutally windy conditions (I was there in Barrakaldo, Bilbao, as the hefty gusts carried away small domestic pets) he summarized "Every lap it was like the devil farting in your face".

Less straightforward was the implication of Spanish endurance legend Marta Dominguez in the doping ring known as Operacion Puerta. She was proven to have dealt in Performance Enhancing Drugs (PEDs) though not definitively to have actually taken any herself. She continued a long and hugely successful career until her mid-30s and somewhat conveniently the ensuing ban came with her first pregnancy and retirement from the sport. She was a huge role model across women's sport well beyond performance running and the negative press coverage of her comeuppance seemed highly diluted compared to what would happen if a British athlete of such status was banned in such circumstances. The president of the Federation, who for many years seemed in practice to operate far more in line with a CEO role, said in an interview, regarding whether Dominguez had actually used PEDs "only she can say the truth when her hand is in the fire".

Individuals' ethics aside, in recent years a trio of Spanish city marathons have made major inroads into the fastest and most intensely front-loaded events in the world. Seville, Barcelona, and Valencia, held in February, March and December respectively have capitalised on their reliable and ideal seasonal weather trends, and their long, wide and very flat city roads. To these advantages they've added city council backing and large corporate support, a solid national base and public interest in high level performance and they lay on some of the world's best events.

Indeed, Valencia has as its city's corporate strapline "Ciudad de correr" (City of Running) and backs up its road race jamboree with separate world class events at 10k and half marathon. To top this, it even has a customised 400 metres athletics track deliberately built slightly below surrounding street level to reduce any wind, and thus it was the chosen venue for Joshua Cheptegei's barely comprehensible world 10,000 metres record of 26.11 set in autumn 2020, one of the rare sporting highlights in the depths of covid lockdown.

Against this grand trio Madrid doesn't have a prayer. Hilly, pitched at 600 metres altitude, held in late April when the weather is starting to heat up, and with its citizenry so selfish that they expect visitors to tolerate them using Spanish as their given language, it focuses on quantity rather than quality in its major marathon.

My niche reading has left me with a somewhat warped range of Spanish vocabulary such that I can rattle off no end of trivia about training but really struggle to name some basic items. It's thus always disappointing in a tapas bar when the waiter, once the patatas bravas con salsa y tortilla are ordered, shows no interest in discussing half marathon pacing strategies. And the local plumber didn't find that the banter about the European 10,000 metres Challenge enabled any better understanding of why the shower kept leaking. I've learned over the years that "struggling with the Spanish subjunctive " is the lesser known third strand of the "death and taxes" axiom regarding the two certainties of life.

In 2002 a combination of this interest in Spanish things, a strong preference for warmth over cold, for daylight over darkness and for quiet villages over vast cities led me to stump up for a very basic little house in the Sierras about 40 miles northeast of Malaga. Even the house purchase nudge came directly from a running link. I was at a new off the beaten track training camp near Lake Vinuela, amongst the first dozen visitors of a programme set up by an emigre from Yorkshire who had a long background in semi-pro cycling. He happened to be selling his Spanish house at the time and as part of one day out he took us there and mentioned the price. By any comparison with the South of England it was an extremely low sum. It had three bedrooms and two receptions so I dug around to see what a two bed one reception place in the same beautiful village would cost. (Smug self-satisfied trigger warning). Having viewed his place in mid-March I completed the purchase of my place down the road in late June and with all taxes and costs included I had change from £40k. My daughter was then about ten months old and as she chowed down another bowl of mashed chicken and turnip the concept of student debt was a very nebulous can which we could in due course start to kick along a road as long as Route 66. The exchange rate at the time was 1.63 Euros to the Pound and that was decisive in shifting from pipedream to purchase.

The views from the roof terrace are priceless and always lift whatever passes for my soul, with the mountains of the Sierra ranges in one direction soaring right behind the village (which sits 700 metres above sea level) and the valley carving down to the coast, 20 kilometres due south, in the other direction. The village, whilst very much on the hilly side for structured running, is prime cycling territory and is regularly used on the professional Tour of Andalucia and periodically in La Vuelta, the major Tour of Spain. I joke that the house itself is of minimal interest or use and that really it's only the terrace that I want, though in spite of giving up physics at age 13 I just about grasp that a roof has to have something to be the roof of.

If you enjoy the extended daylight in southern Spain (sunset on the shortest day of December 20th is around 6.15pm, whilst in Northern

England it's dusk shortly after you've put the lunch rubbish in the recycling bin) you have Franco's political affiliation to Hitler to be grateful for. Although you'd maybe do best not to word it quite that way. Spain is in the "wrong " time zone. It should be aligned with the UK and Ireland but out of respect for the Germans in the late 1930s Franco set Spanish time to align with that of Germany and the nations they were invading, though based on its location Spain ought to lie one hour west of them.

A serendipitous browse in the village's weekly street market unearthed a harriers gem. There is a charity book stall selling off second hand volumes at one Euro each. Mostly it's airport schlock but one unexpected nugget I picked up was "The Road to Athens" by British star of the 1960s Bill Adcocks. The title refers to his legendary win over the notoriously tough Athens marathon course in 1967 in a then world class time of 2.11.07. This gave him the number one world ranking that year and remarkably the time stood as a course record for several decades, even outlasting the 2004 Olympics in Athens when Italian Stefano Baldini triumphed in a slightly slower time (albeit in sticky conditions). The book, (and I was so delighted to chance upon it that I didn't even haggle over the price) was published to synch with those Athens Games and was knocked into good readable shape by the late Trevor Frecknall, an old breed sports journalist just as Adcocks was a real old school enduro. And if gazing down training plans and mileage tables isn't quite your thing, then there's illuminating material around the social and economic history of the West Midlands; Adcocks slotted in his mileage - of which there was a lot - around a full-time job as a gas fitter. Post retirement age Adcocks worked for a while for UK Athletics as a communications officer and I'd speculate he might also have been useful if the HQ kettle needed a new fuse.

As I drafted this chapter, in short order two of the Spanish elites, both of Moroccan birth, received doping bans. One was a global star, Mo Katir, who made huge progress from 1500 to 5000 metres just after the covid era and swept up the already exceptional Spanish records at these events. He missed three 'whereabouts' random tests – that is, not being at the 'official' address when unannounced dope testers arrived. This, although not actually a positive test, 'counts' as a doping violation. The other was a lesser light but was a regular on the Spanish team on track and cross country. Even his coach, the abovementioned Serrano, described how he found his conduct suspicious, training away from the elite Madrid group and making trips to Ifrane in Morocco.

Perhaps even more alarming in that it could suggest some deep-rooted ethical 'weakness' in endurance sport, rather than a couple of errant individuals, was an extraordinary case in cycle racing. At a semi pro/amateur and club level 90k road race in Vinalopo, in the Valencia region, very shortly before the start time the Spanish anti-doping agency announced that random dope testing would operate at the event. At a stroke 80 out of 132 entrants suddenly withdrew. One can say that the cycling culture isn't the same as that of running and there's some truth in that given cycling's doping history over the last century but with the growth of triathlon and duathlon we aren't looking at a totally separate set of values or participants. It's also possible that with marijuana and cocaine as banned drugs albeit of no performance benefit, several of the "no participar" absconders were recreational users. But still, it doesn't help the perception of the sport.

7

COACHING, COACHES, COACHEES

Introduction and Old Style 'Influencers'

This long section is partly ordered and structured, and partly episodic and may even appear scattergun. Before you think that this is just sloppy writing and editing, it's actually a good mirror for how coaching seems to work in practice, over time, and coach by coach, as this chapter considers. Sticking to strict chronological order would not be the best way to present what has happened and - strange as it may sound – would likely make things look more disordered. Some episodes are just that – little standalone incidents which after twenty years and – by a rough calculation – some 15,000 to 20,000 hours of time that falls within coaching, still carry resonance, for the better (usually) or very occasionally the worse.

The one overriding aspect not to be overlooked is that coaches coach because we like it. Just as runners don't like every run that they do, when they may often be tired, battling the cold, wind or rain (indeed all three simultaneously fairly frequently in the UK). But like the sport's fulfilment, so it is with coaches. We have to turn up whatever the weather, whatever the traffic or train strike scenario may be. We have to reply to challenging communications and situations that we would much rather not have to face. Unless we are very lucky or have flawless judgement of character, we'll likely be treated very poorly by someone we coach at some stage. But we like contributing. At least a part of is that everyone likes to have a clear purpose; indeed, at some level, to feel important, whether it be as head of a national federation or guiding an Under 15 to score in their club's team. Of course, it has to be much more than that.

Amidst the narrative there are some standalone profiles of various memorable and outstanding people I've known as runners who I have coached or coaches I've encountered. I had no idea these people existed when I started coaching. Indeed, I'm now just about at the stage where I'll be coaching people who actually didn't exist when I started out. (Quite possibly when they try to do the last chunky block of some gruelling Threshold session I've tasked them with they'll be wishing I didn't exist too). In a way that I never articulate – or really think about, outside drafting this text – stepping away from the sport would be cutting off the chance to continue these links and life would be undoubtedly a duller thing to live.

Literally the first coaching dialogue I had, once I had made the decision, was with someone who I had known for years and found them to be a less than inspiring figure, but as usual they were at the track on my Day One. Their opening line was "I see myself more as a facilitator of athlete performance than a coach" which just confirmed my view that we would not become tight coaching buddies.

By luck I started when the Governing Body was revamping its coaching qualification curriculum and, just as importantly, the support structures and people and resources it offered. Amongst numerous debates that it threw up was, within the pages of Athletics Weekly, a difference of opinion between two well-known voices within the endurance world, those of world class marathon runner Mara Yamauchi, who took a supportive stance and the excellent writer, runner and all-round pundit Will Cockerill who said it as he saw it and was not overly impressed with some aspects.

The further you head into coaching, the smaller a proportion of your total coaching body of knowledge and development comes directly from the official curriculum. That's not a problem in any way nor any criticism of the formal courses. It's surely a given for a keen coach to be proactive about their development and not for the governing body to micromanage the details of how they go about this.

In old money and simplifying for the purpose at hand, it had 4 levels.

• Level 1 was real bare bones generic safety first. It seems to start from the premise that the new coach may have no experience whatsoever of the sport, or of dealing with coaching processes in life outside sport, or of taking responsibility for others. Of course, most new coaches will not be quite so raw so there's an element of politely going through the motions. It will take maybe one or two days out of your life, and you'll have some fun. It's the smallest of small beer if you are planning to coach long term.

• Level 2 meant you could be insured to independently and competently coach a session in your event group (such as sprints, endurance, jumps, throws).

• Level 3 meant you could provide individual training plans and ongoing training advice in your event group as well as suitable sessions for groups and individuals.

• Level 4, as the highest, meant you could do everything for the highest level of athlete in your chosen event within the event group. And within your event group you had to show specialisation at one event – I chose 10,000 metres partly because it's a fascinating event and partly to guard against being unduly identified as a marathon coach. Fat lot of good that did.

One notable face-to-face on this last module was a truly helpful session with Jeremy Harries, then one of England Athletics' leading coach educators and assessors, who had travelled down from North West England to pick apart my coaching 'philosophy'. The very word 'philosophy' can seem self-important when applied to coaching. After all, one doesn't ask a 5k runner or a track referee their philosophy regarding their chosen role in the sport. But philosophy can be defined as "the study of the theoretical basis of a particular branch of knowledge or experience" or "a theory or attitude that acts as a guiding principle for behaviour". So it seems a reasonable description though Plato or Bertrand Russell might have seen it as dumbing down from weightier options.

It was not an easy dialogue as Jeremy went to the core of my motives and wouldn't swallow anything sounding slightly woolly or insincere or box ticking. Eventually I came out with words to the effect that I liked seeing people succeed at their maximum level and wished to be in a position to be a relevant part of that success and he accepted that and mentioned that this chimed with his own principles. His own coaching pedigree, primarily through Preston Harriers, included the developmental years of the likes of Helen Clitheroe, and now herself a leading high performance coach and the late John Nuttall, a fellow Olympian and Commonwealth Games medallist, and who still sits very high on the UK All time lists for 3000 metres, and who also pursued a professional coaching career within UK Athletics.

This structure is in theory designed to give a generic framework of quality assurance to capture all the niches and strands of coaching in the sport across age groups, levels of talent and commitment. Which is one of the reasons why so little heed is given at ground level to which level a particular coach is qualified at. Many runners dealing with an experienced won't know or care. It would be comparable to asking a Doctor what grade they had in A Level biology.

I thought the structure was broadly fine as it was and within all the contextual factors of Governing Body budgets and coaches' own enthusiasm and planning. Sometimes is seemed that some coaches had naïve and unrealistic expectations of what the Governing Body should be doing for them, versus what they should be doing for themselves. There were also frequent objections to the cost of the courses and resources. At the time, the mid to late 2000s, the total financial cost of covering the Levels 1 to 4 was around £1000, unlikely to be condensed into less than five or six years. In nearly all cases this would be covered by a coach's club if the coach was providing some volunteer coaching within the club. And for those few coaches who were only coaching on a commercial basis (this part of coaching has moved on, as I describe below), this modest sum was a tax-deductible expense. Compared to any other sort of qualification or professional development that one can gain, I never thought the costs worthy of the debate that they stirred up.

Reflecting the shifting and widening constituency of 'endurance running' there is also a Coach in Running Fitness qualification which has comparable standing to Athletics Coach in Endurance but is tilted towards adult recreational running. Predictably, there is considerable and evolving overlap in how these licenced coaches operate.

Bud Baldaro was the first coach within the official athletics structure who gave me the opportunity to start moving beyond a single local club atmosphere and invited me to the UKA marathon squad weekends through 2004 to 2006 where with the most parsimonious budget he put on some great events for athletes and coaches. A mixture of tough training sessions and interviews and seminars. Nothing groundbreaking and within the set-up, resources and location it wasn't really primarily intended to delve into sports science minutiae. But as a mix of information and inspiration and – for the athletes – tough endurance sessions that offered tight group running with peers that they did not all have at their home-town clubs, it was very well designed. It had at least some role in nudging the likes of Dan Robinson and Mara Yamauchi towards their successes at international and up to Olympic level.

Bud had been in the sport for decades and had been a fine runner (faster than he would admit to unless pressed) and had been an English teacher in, mainly, Reading though had always retained his deep West Midlands brogue. He had coached literally scores of international runners down the years and covered the full gamut from middle distance to marathon.

He had long had a working link with Birmingham University, in latter years being employed there as a coach, once returning to the area and many of his coachees were Birmingham alumni. He had huge numbers of people demanding of his time with the various roles he covered. He would typically have three mobile phones to hand; one for personal use; one for Birmingham Uni duties and a third for governing body communication and they seemed to be almost constantly buzzing and chiming. I noticed that he was a sharp assessor of how quickly and effectively people could make good use of whatever words he offered in response. Hence, he seemed to have evolved a kind of verbal shorthand to give people a few snippets of advice or information and let them fill in the missing words and roll on as needed. He was my official mentor with England Athletics, and I've always felt very lucky on that front. Two of the three National endurance mentors had lengthy coaching CVs at the highest level including several Olympians and the third, and slightly younger, Martin Rush, had actually been an Olympian, in 1992 and then had a classic career pathway in athlete performance management once his peak competition years were over.

Area Coach Mentoring

It suits my narrative to draw the following correlation but if one traces the decline and gradual reemergence of British endurance standards in depth there is a case that the lowest depths were around 2003 to 2006 and that the setting up of the national coaching mentoring and development scheme coincided with standards picking up again. Also undoubtedly in the mix was the huge growth of content on the internet which gave people access to best practice, albeit not every item of training content on the internet is best practice.

One of the area mentors was the North Eastern legend, the late Lyndsay Dunn who had been behind the immense Gateshead success of the 1970s and 1980s, famously Brendan Foster and Charlie Spedding, both Olympic medallists, plus a long sequence of other internationals. Across the Pennines in the North West was the down to earth Stan Taylor, whose running CV included a 3.58 mile in the very early 1960s when such a feat was truly international class; and he'd just missed out on England selection for what was the last Empire Games, before it was rebranded as the Commonwealth Games.

Undeniably several other factors have been in play and it was true – as occasional columns in Athletics Weekly would show - that some of the older guard of coaches weren't so enamoured with the new coaching structures and opportunities (in my mid 40s I was frequently described by some of the eminences gris as a young man) but for the period of my involvement I found it immensely helpful and fulfilling.

The Area Coach Mentoring was a novel role. Aside from the core purpose, of working individually with a group of coaches in the area, and organising training events/coaching seminars for coaches and athletes to attend, there was an illuminating insight into the nation's private vs public bureaucracy cultures. Those of us, including myself, with public sector working backgrounds, found the admin and reporting demands sensibly and refreshingly light whereas those from the private sector grouched about the excessive amount of formfilling. That aside, the set up as it existed for five years (nine Area mentors given small part time roles, working to the three National mentors and - trust me on this - correspondingly small fees) was designed to be an optimal use of people's time. As a superficial example, if a team meeting was scheduled for a 9.00 start and you walked in at 9.05 you'd have missed something of substance.

The role gave access to some coaching pow wows that I might otherwise not have been at. Shortly after London 2012 the late UKA performance director Neil Black hosted a session focused on the factors that contributed to Mo Farah's success, at a stage when he had piled up 'just' three of what would become an unsurpassable ten global golds by 2017. He opened up by asking the floor to pipe up with key factors and he joked with an element of relief when UKA itself was eventually offered as about the 6th contributor. Obviously, the Nike Oregon Project in the USA, to which Farah relocated in 2010/11, was flagged up early and there was also a view, subjective but not unfounded, that prodigious potential track runners were bypassing the 5000 and 10,000 and moving early in their elite careers straight to marathon and half marathon for primarily financial reasons. Given the speed of the elite track performances being totted up by the worlds fastest since Farah retired from the track, particularly at 5000 metres, it's a questionable point of view unless he just happened to luck out with 'weak' opponents in a 6-year window, an unlikely pattern.

The populist narrative (Britain seems to be big on populist narratives in various walks of life) continually underplays quite how outstandingly good he was before he moved to Oregon. His PBs when USA-based progressed by barely one per cent but the game changer, that one per cent aside, was the development in his late race change of pace both for the final 1000 metres and within that, the bell lap of 400 metres. One doesn't need to be a biomechanics expert to see that his movement pattern at his peak was more finely honed than previously. This was coupled with incredibly astute race positioning as the laps unfolded and with this came huge mental confidence. That cheesy but not inaccurate "owning the start line" phrase was heard frequently in the Farah era. This correlated, it could seem from watching the opposition, with a corresponding decline in confidence amongst his likeliest rivals, both in their body language and how they let the races unfold.

At another gathering, Black gave an illuminating presentation on how physios could optimally work with high level distance runners and coaches. He was arguably the best placed person in the world to comment on this liaison as, following his own outstanding career as a junior which was curtailed by injury, he trained as a physio, grew a tremendous reputation from his base in Epsom, then gained employment in the new English Institute of Sport when Lottery funding kicked in. From this pan-sport position he moved to the Performance Director role within UKA. Amongst the many hundreds who had received his treatment was yours truly, who was once on the couch where as I walked in Tony Jarrett, world silver medallist at 100m hurdles, left his treatment and as I left the rather more finely honed aerobic figure of Sonia O Sullivan strolled in for treatment. Black gave me an extensive set of rehab drills to do two or three times daily in the immediate period after a meniscus operation. This memory came back during his presentation when he self-deprecatingly mentioned that sometimes a focused physio can slightly lose track of how athletes operate in the real world. He related how a female runner had asked when or if she might scale back the battery of drills he had given her for her rehab, because the daily sequence was taking over 3 hours daily...... In his Performance Director role at UKA he was where the buck stopped in the World and Olympic Championships medal count and so became more of a politician and senior manager than a hands on practitioner.

A couple of years earlier another meeting had what I thought some less enthralling moments. The main content was from a senior UK federation official in the endurance sector, who was a former world class runner. In the course of setting out where improvements could be made, they said how tactically badly a certain Brit had run in a global track final the previous year - whilst that runner's coach was in the meeting; then came the opinion that another British distance runner, who had already medalled at the European Cross Country champs "definitely" needed a new coach (the then-current coach should have been in the meeting but was late); then opined that if a certain Brit did not win the following year's European Championship at their chosen track event, they needed a "doctor for [their]head". The athlete didn't manage this and was on record with mental health issues down the years. Once these athletes had been reeled off, the officer then went on to the support staff - naming one of the key sports science team and saying that they weren't world class and would need replacing. I noted down this catalogue of critiques which I thought was oddly indiscreet and unprofessional.

Coaches
Stella Bandu – Exploiting Kentish Gems

One of my first coaching contacts from outside the North London area was Stella Bandu. We first met at London's South Bank University to chew the London endurance fat with coaching guru Geoff Williams and the one off, and now much missed, Bob Smith, the England Athletics Area Manager. Bob lived and breathed the sport and for a former national level high jumper knew a great deal about the endurance events. His father had been a legendary 400 metres coach down in the Solent area with the likes of Todd Bennett, Kris Akabussi and Paul Sanders amongst many elite one lappers he coached. Bob's immense knowledge acquired over, literally, his entire life came with a great wit and warm personable nature and the governing body struck lucky in having him as its representative in the capital. Sadly he died young, having just reached sixty and with so much more left to offer.

Although born in Kent Stella's family history was somewhat atypical and she traces her own resilience and persistence through their travails. Specifically, her father who was a student in Romania, was friends with the children of UK embassy officials and his father was a wealthy self-made businessman, while the nation was in its era of severe Soviet communism.

He was arrested, accused of spying and spent thirteen years in a Bucharest prison through his 20s and 30s for the crime of not supporting communism and was tortured during his period of incarceration. Indeed it was only through the good luck (using those two words very flexibly here) of having a doctor as a fellow prisoner that he survived the spell, including surgery to remove his appendix. Medical facilities were minimal, and operations were conducted with limited equipment and only local anaesthetic.

He was released in the early 1960s as part of an amnesty and flown at almost no notice to the UK. After living in London for a while he married her mother and moved to the Isle of Sheppey. Stella was born on Sheppey and much of the Romanian heritage filtered through to her over the years. Her mother became one of the earliest Church of England women priests in the country, another unusual note on the family's collective CV.

She had no particular sporting prowess; she started some recreational distance running as a student at the then Bristol Polytechnic (a four-year degree in town and country planning which became her long term career in Kent) and then joined Ashford AC near the Kent coast. She did the typical club mix of cross country and road races and completed three big city marathons in times that she keeps under wraps (and may indeed have forgotten). She struggled with injuries in her late 20s and, in her word which is echoed by so many coaches, "drifted" into coaching. She is always keen to stress that a lot of her coaching practice and style is rooted in generic skills and approaches that she developed in her working career.

Initially it was leading warm up exercises and drills and then things evolved, and she coached the club's middle-distance youngsters in the Under 13 and Under 15 group. Kent has always been a strong running county and historically the biggest clubs in the county had drawn in the leading endurance talents from smaller clubs. For some years it was Invicta East Kent and in the last 25 to 30 years the mantle of Kent running powerhouse has passed to Tonbridge.

The particular athlete whose talent and arrival at age 13 into Stella's orbit was Lisa Dobriskey. She was a standout from an early age at 800/1500 and cross country, the classic endurance mix at that age. She did group sessions with the club's quicker boys of her age. Although she incurred a stress fracture in her mid-teens this was, in the wider years of progress, but a small glitch and with Stella's ongoing guidance she made the immense step of qualifying for UK selection for the World Under 20 championships in 2002 in Kingston, Jamaica. A tall local chap named Usain featured somewhat in the men's sprints whilst Dobriskey excelled to place 4th in the women's 1500 metres. This was shortly before she started her English degree at Loughborough. In the years up to the World Juniors Stella had had numerous "outreach " coaching development opportunities taking her outside the local club remit. She says "I was lucky " in that she received mentoring from some of the leading coaching luminaries of the time such as Conrad Milton, Neville Taylor, and UK steeplechase record holder (currently 36 years and counting) and Olympic medallist Mark Rowland and in particular she developed her skills in movement, strength and conditioning.

Gradually the coaching transition for Lisa D meant that the legendary George Gandy at Loughborough (where one way or another he was for several decades employed by the university and the UK federation in various guises) assumed her coaching responsibility. Building on the established CV Dobriskey had achieved, she went on to World Championship silver in 2009 and two Commonwealth gold medals plus two Olympic finals, all at 1500.

Shortly after this Stella was handpicked by the UKA Cross Country team managers to carry out this role for the GB Under 20 women (Teams of six was the norm) at European and then World Championships level. This lasted four years and gave numerous memorable experiences and the relevant teams' results certainly suggests that they were well managed.

A more sustained involvement with a similar level of female athletes occurred over the 2005 to 2012 era via the well-known On Camp With Kelly programme. This was essentially Kelly Holmes' legacy to the sport, and specifically to young women's middle distance running after her own career had dramatically peaked with the double Olympic gold in 800 and 1500 in Athens, some of the modern era's most memorable sporting moments from a UK perspective.

She had planned to retire post Athens (and her age, 34, just adds to how remarkable the achievements were) and the "legacy " programme was in her "retirement plan" anyway but the double gold raised its profile and indeed its resources. Aviva, the insurance company who were then UKA's biggest funder were pleased to support the programme as was the Federation itself. Indeed, given that 800 and 1500m fall within the endurance sector in which the longer distances were increasingly being monopolized by East African athletes, it made strategic sense to channel resources to the middle distances where the leading global lights were more evenly spread across nations. Holmes provided overall leadership and inspiration and some ground level expertise at strength and conditioning in particular (linked to the job she had held in the Army for some years before making the step to full time athletics) and a small team of managers, sports science and medicine experts and coaches including Stella were recruited to give the programme ongoing professionalism and quality assurance. One could say that it was like an event specific Lottery programme tailored for the age group it supported of mainly 16- to 21-year-olds. At full capacity 50 runners were on the programme including a few young men in the later years. Some went onto global senior championship success such as Hannah England, Laura Weightman, Charlotte Purdue and Non Stanford so the full range of 800 metres to marathon plus world class triathlon was embraced later in their careers, another indicator of the long term benefits of avoiding specialising too early. And inevitably given the life choices that youngsters make, a few dropped out before the senior ranks.

She believes that the national coach development that occurred via invited athletes often bringing their home coaches was a legacy of the Camp, as also was a big step forward in the awareness, particularly among male coaches, of the specifics of coaching girls and women.

Stella also became immersed in steeplechase development. This long-distance hurdles race is contested over 3000 metres for both genders, and 2000m for under 20s. It was a late addition to the women's programme at global level since the late 1990s so over the last 20 years the women's event has substantially improved in depth internationally yet it's fair to say that, with a couple of notable exceptions, the UK remains outside the world's leading players even outside East Africa. She describes the ever-present logistical issues of doing steeplechase sessions at a track, in that you can't put out barriers whilst any other groups are using the track, otherwise you will be compelling them to clear or run around them! "Expect The Unexpected" is a useful prompt but it has its limits. This practical hindrance is aside from the sheer difficulty of persuading distance runners to try, and then to stick with this event. It has in many ways become a self-fulfilling cycle with very few ex-steeplechasers, very few steeplechase coaches and so very little to make it an alluring prospect for any but a very small minority. At elite level it is every bit as exciting to watch as any other distance race. Indeed, with the jeopardy, visual variation and drama of the water jump it is arguably more compelling. It is undeniably a technically difficult event requiring at higher level a very skilled technical base to integrate with the running demands. (At Spring 2024 it is almost 40 years since a British male runner attained what is the 2024 Olympic qualifying time at the event, so anyone achieving it will be literally a once in a generation achiever.)

In recent years, showing that sometimes in coaching things happen to you beyond what you directly seek, Stella's core group at Ashford has become a group of 17- to 22-year-old guys. It's a notably high-level group with a sprinkling of England and GB under 20 internationals and others at county to national level. And given her profile, runners from clubs beyond Ashford increasingly fall within her coaching radar. In a favourable coincidence of timing, Stella was able to step back from full time employment a few years ago when indeed her "full time" role became the byzantine administration of her late uncle's Romanian and USA estate which eventually enabled her to manage without ongoing work demands. Hence the massive amount of her time channelled to all things coaching, including some project-based consultancy work with talented young athletes. This draws on her particular combination of technical knowledge of the sport and general workplace skills and experience and empathy with the mid to late teen age groups. Perhaps no surprise her husband is an equally committed high jump coach.

Dave Newport

The charismatic one-off character of coach Dave Newport came onto my radar via the long since defunct University Athletics forum (formerly eightlane.com) where we both posted diligently in all weathers, and notwithstanding that our combined ages of over 80 were towards the upper end of its users. He posted as DaveN and I as dc3, because I'd had too many incorrect logins as dc1 and dc2. My banking login is dc954 for this same reason, which is largely why I keep a large stash of £20 notes in the kitchen in a little gap behind the rice jar.

Anyway, Dave came across as a fount of wisdom and opinions and with a lively and witty style and so I sought him out to discover the person behind the postings. He's one of the most driven and impressive self-educated people you might meet. He told me how he'd " canned school at 15" and then spent some 15 years in the army (not actually joining at 15; the Conservative government of the 1980s did indeed whittle away at workers' rights but not quite this far). On leaving he had gone into a private security role so hush hush they he himself didn't know who the client was. He worked unusual shift hours which gave him plenty of free time in most days, and thus the fulfilling opportunity to post on a message board about athletics. Though as he describes below, he was hugely committed on the coaching at ground level – with countless thousands of road miles to carry this out. He had done very well in his day job, and one could see why. Quick thinking, an articulate talker, fine organiser, and ability to relate to a wide range of people. He was quite a phone chatterer and after one of the frequent calls he made to me at home my 6-year-old daughter asked the left field non sequitur "Are you gay with Dave N?" I thought at the time that whilst her Haringey junior school had clearly finessed their citizenship and inclusion classes for Year 2 it was a shame they had totally sidelined Latin.

On one such call, as we spoke Dave suddenly saw his jeans spinning round the inner barrel of the washing machine and realised his wife had put these in with over £200 cash in his pockets, which would thus be wrecked beyond useable recognition. He was incredibly unbothered by this and barely interrupted his flow to point this out.

As things unfolded, I partnered with Dave to set up our first paid coaching website around the late 2000s. In theory it had potential but then Dave realised that at this time he had an unshakeable resistance to accepting payment for his coaching. This extended even to a family cosseted in the heart of London's Belgravia having their son advised by the maestro. You'll spot here that the financial returns of refusing any revenue are not the rosiest.

I hadn't seen Dave for some while and then one Tuesday evening at a Serpentine session I heard, whilst standing in the weakly floodlit patch by the 200 metres point, a disembodied voice calling "Hey, short guy with glasses, get off the track when you're coaching ". For a second I looked around for this obnoxious interloper and then the west country burr clicked my recall button and I explained to the Serpie crew that, contrary to first impression, Dave was an impeccably well-mannered guru of the sport. But the very large majority of has career has had no link with me, so he can enlighten us as follows below.

He started "by accident", at Cirencester AC, when the junior group coach left at short notice, and he took up the slack for a few weeks, having himself just transitioned to the senior group that summer. At this stage he was a national level judo player, but used running for training and had run decent track times, "so I was happy to help out with something I enjoyed doing. In the 1980s, if you were any good, you'd find yourself coaching younger kids, at almost every judo training session, so I think that this helped me A LOT when starting to coach runners."

Four years on and the stop gap role was still in place – quite a long time to plug a gap - and Dave had built "a tidy group of kids, who were regularly making it to English Schools Athletics Champs over 400-3000 metres. One of those kids turns 50 this summer and he's been with me since 1986...possibly some kind of bizarre endurance/torture record. I have so many stories of the kind of things that we got up to in that group."

As I haven't checked the sport's welfare policies from the late 1980s nor the precise details of the timelines for applying the statute of limitations, it is worth emphasising that at no time did Dave's coachees ever sleep rough in London train stations before races nor did they hitchhike to races in Europe. ("Hitch hiking" - for the benefit of younger readers - was a practice that involved climbing into a car with a total stranger and expecting that when they dropped you at your destination their behavioural record remained just as it had been when you started the journey).

Aged 20 he joined the army, with the full intention of being an almost full-time judo player, having been told that Judo was a well-supported army sport. On arrival at his first unit in York, he discovered that everybody on the team was being posted out, so he switched to the track and cross-country teams instead. This allowed him to train twice a day, as this unit were Army champions for both track and cross country at the time. Running regular 50-70 mile weeks he soon discovered that "my Achilles wasn't having any of it" and he wasn't going to make any impact in that team, so he focussed on progressing the coaching. He helped some middle-distance types to 800 metre times of 1:53-1:56 and some road/country types get down to 31-32 minutes, with one of the local civvies running sub 30 minutes for 10k and 65 for half marathon.

After four years in York, he had to choose "whether to take a fairly random posting or leave the army, so I chose neither and signed up for the selection course in Hereford. The first four weeks consist of 4-6 hours solo navigation, point to point, across the Brecon Beacons, carrying a house on your back, staying within the cutoff times, to stay on the course. Obviously, coming from a running and judo background, I was capable of this, but Jesus Christ, it was horrendous, as I simply wasn't conditioned for it. This led to the final endurance march [which has a worrying whiff of mortality in its title], which was advertised as 64 km, but as that's the point-to-point measurement on an OS map, the reality is a lot longer, taking in every grim peak they could find. I decided to change my socks, due to hotspots on my feet. I was within two hours of the finish, so there was no danger of me missing the cutoff. Boot off, sock off, but the sole of my foot was stuck to it, so sole off, from the heel to ball of my foot. The next four hours were a nightmare, as I hobbled and cried all the way in.... I don't cry over many things (mostly just funerals), but this was the worst pain I'd been in.... broken by a bit of a blister. Got round though, thankfully inside the cutoff time." So, to Hereford, where he spent the next nine years.

"On arrival, the local club gave me seven lads whom they saw as the least talented/worst behaved kids they had, and laughed. After a few years, all but one of them had made it to the English Schools Track & Field Championships.......so, lack of talent wasn't really the problem after all. They just needed to be given a bit of purpose, some good training and have somebody believe in them, whilst supporting them endlessly. If nothing else, I'm pretty good at supporting athletes through every challenge."

"That group outgrew the club, so we moved over to Cheltenham Harriers in 2001. Cheltenham were failing to produce Under 20/ Senior athletes, so I steadily built a group, that turned into our Harriers endurance group." Over this era Dave was also delving into duathlon as he had some cycling background and some of his coaching charges were heading that way. He spent several years as GB Elite Duathlon/Long Distance Triathlon team manager at European and World level events.

"I moved down to Somerset in 2018 but have continued to travel up to Cheltenham/Hereford training sessions (at my own expense) each week, as I love it.

Almost 4 years ago, after Cheltenham had NEVER had an athlete from the club's junior group progress up to the senior group, I made some proposals to address the issue. These went well at committee level, but when they didn't actually carry out any of the required actions, I left, to set up what is now the glorious Western Tempo Running Club. I thought that I'd be leaving with a loyal handful, so I was surprised when I actually left with 70 senior athletes, leaving just 5 or 6 Harriers stalwarts at the club. From there, it's been a blast."

And unsurprisingly they quickly became one of the Midlands region's heavy hitters (winning the Area's 12 stage Road Relay Championship in 2024) and are starting to perform well nationally. Leading one club from the front is not quite enough for him so he taken on the endurance coaching as a volunteer for Exeter University who are thriving.

He is a great motivator at coaxing runners to realise what they may be able to achieve provided they put the work in and play the long game and his main sessions are high on aerobic oomph and volume. This isn't the only consideration, but once the coach knows the runner has built their evening around the group session, plus return travel to the venue, the default should be that they work pretty darned hard, using the group vibe to push each other on.

George Loucaides – Nicosian Nuances

Cypriot Under 20 Javelin throwers aren't usually the obvious source to seek out valuable and illuminating endurance coaching links. But that's the unpredictable nature of life and is also why I preciously insist that I coach in the sport of athletics rather than the leisure activity of running.

Some years ago, I started coaching Demetrios Z as he gradually progressed his distance running in his mid-40s from a fairly moderate starting base. His main previous sporting prowess had been as a late teens javelin thrower, winging it out close to 70 metres and becoming a junior Cyprus international and then a Blue at Cambridge. He is surely the most accomplished javelin thrower I've ever coached and I suggested at the outset that the explosivity he used at that event, fast twitch dominated as it was, probably meant that he veered towards a lesser potential at long distance running. He has always persevered amidst a hectic professional life which I'll simplify to Entrepreneur in Technology. His post Cambridge CV shifted to Harvard and McKinsey so suffice to say he's quite the achiever.

In early 2024 he mentioned that he was about to have standard physiological tests (VO2 max plus anaerobic threshold plus, in this case, running economy) done in Cyprus and he knew the lab tester, who had recently coached a long term coachee to a big new Cypriot national marathon record of 2.10.20 in his debut at the event. It was maybe no surprise that it was the 2.10 marathon coaching strand that I pounced on.

And so I had the first zoom meeting with George Loucaides in Nicosia. He has the most minuscule online footprint which always warms my old school heart. But not because there's nothing to show. In 1991 he was European Under 20 steeplechase champion, twice running 8 minutes 45 seconds that year (which was the 4th fastest Junior time in the world that year), so he was a real talent from a relative backwater nation. This earned him an athletic scholarship to Washington State University, always a big hitter in the NCAA endurance world and in those days having strong links with Kenyan runners. Indeed, its Kenyan liaison had gained a very high early profile as Henry Rono had attended there in the late 1970s at his record-breaking peak, and several of his countrymen followed over the years.

George had followed the sports science path through to PhD level and focused on Exercise Physiology. Currently, serving a Cypriot population of just 1.2 million, he has a varied professional and coaching life which, perhaps coincidentally, matches some of my past. He coaches a range of long-distance runners, from elite through strong club level to more moderate standards, and provides physiological testing via the institute at which he works. He is also involved in a more managerial way in advising and implementing on general physical activity programmes for the island, feeding into the European Union policy arena, in the area where public health, sport and leisure overlap.

So, minus the starry athletics past, we share plenty of common ground and he's a dynamic character (so, we don't share that trait), great knowledge, always a good listener and a reflector and ongoing learner. We always have quite focused zooms even if we have no prepared agenda. I think this is partly because we have time constrained meets given that neither of us has upsized from the 40 minute freebie package (and it is very hard to find anyone who has done so outside their workplace setup!) so we see the clock ticking; and partly because neither of us knows the individuals whom the other coaches so we can't get side tracked by digressions, by which I can be tempted when time allows. When we are recalling something from our past running days, and his were very much more glamorous, there's always some coaching point to be gleaned, rather than just nostalgia for its own sake.

I've often heard it said that coaching can be a "lonely " occupation. I've never found this, though I'm on the self-contained end of being fine with my own company; but breaking up the ceaseless flow of emails and WhatsApps with a facetime dialogue in lively company is certainly enriching.

Whilst he's not a miracle worker he does offer a protocol that seems to be effective in preventing cramps in marathons. Yes, that elusive remedy.

We discussed the syndrome and the two big standouts that in most cases it only occurred at the late stages of marathon races, in that rare combination of long distance and hard pace that is almost never encountered in a single training effort. We also observed that it tended to surface when runners were at their limit and arguably running just slightly too fast. I said that I'd gone down the usual rabbit holes to find descriptions, possibilities, observations and suggestions but nothing that really presented as a "prevention".

Without going into detail, and with the caveat that George's sample size for this is still quite small, it involves a heavy two consecutive days of training in which the later stages of the second day's demands come close to what the body faces in the closing miles of a marathon. As he summarises " We observed that, it was the case with some runners who induced moderate fatigue the previous day of the long run, on a muscular level (with mild tempo, 2nd moderate run or / and some high rep, low weight strength training), may have assisted in proving a total stimulus (added to the long run), to prepare the muscles to cope with the later stages of the marathon, without actually causing the wear and tear that a marathon race would actually have on the body. This approach is often implemented, in some way by ultra runners who do double long runs (on back-to-back days) to simulate to a certain degree the level of fatigue that the body and mind are expected to be required to cope with during the ultra. The race is run once on race day!"

Gavin Smith – Africa out of Aldershot

One tenet about coaching is that if you wish to coach at a level above local club level then you need to be in the right environment to make this feasible. This can mean both the geographical location itself and also the broader environmental factors. At a global elite level, the nations of Rwanda, Tanzania and Uganda all share very similar altitude, economic and societal factors with Kenya and to some degree Ethiopia. Yet the evolution of their running cultures and indeed simply number of top runners falls hugely short of Kenya's.

In Britain too one can make or not make one's own coaching luck to some degree.

One of the most unusual and illuminating cases in its trajectory is that of Gavin Smith whose initial coaching pathway went from suburban England to Iten, the hub of the Kenyan world class heartland, in one unprecedented leap

I first met Gavin briefly at a training event and at age 22 he was a very lively, thoughtful and articulate runner. He sported a stylish porkpie hat, a nice sartorial streak in a high mileage guy. He seemed to get his best results at cross country, and as a youngster with the ever-mighty Aldershot Farnham and District club and then a sports science student at the athlete's mecca of Loughborough University he was always surrounded by runners achieving performances beyond his own limits (as context his PBs from his early to mid 20s include 14.47 5k, 31.06 10k and 68.48 Half Marathon). At just 24 years old and, by any definition, very early in any official coaching role, he and his partner (now wife) decided to up sticks and move to Kenya, initially in a tent. They knew the much lower cost of living would enable them to spend several months there without needing to earn anything, with some UK savings to eke out. But it wasn't just generic Kenyan coaching that Gavin was after but rather a working association with arguably the world's leading endurance coach, Italian guru Renato Canova.

From around the late 1990s there were a small number of Italians who had relocated either fully or for part of each year to coach and manage the leading and most promising Kenyans. This small group were either former elite runners and/or coaches from the Italians' own golden endurance era which spanned around a decade from the early 1980s. In some ways it mirrored the achievements and lifecycle, of the Spanish heyday that followed just a few years later. It was also in some cases assisted by doping, as some of the high-achieving athletes have subsequently confirmed. As the typical Italian lifestyle shifted with increased affluence and decreased physical activity, national endurance prowess predictably dipped and so those working at the sharp end saw Kenyan opportunities growing as the Italian talent pool shrank. Simplistically, applying European science, management, planning and monitoring to the more intuitive Kenyan practices to produce faster individuals, longer careers and of course better rewarded runners. Canova was at the heart of the Kenyans taking over the marathon in the way they had a decade or two earlier taken over the 5000, 10000 and most emphatically of all the 3000m steeplechase. Canova covered the full endurance spectrum with his coaching.

At barely a week's notice Gavin set himself up from Day One as Canova's initially pro bono assistant coach. Indeed, his Loughborough credentials carried such clout that he almost immediately was given the role of coordinating the runners' strength programmes.

Listening to Gavin describe his time there he does not particularly expound on running training minutiae, which with internet access is all out there anyway, as was already largely the case when he arrived in 2010. Canova himself has posted various series of training minutiae on the letsrun.com forum and been graciously willing to discuss these with engaged participants. Most recently, he added to the forum with sixteen weeks of detailed training which Britain's Emile Cairess carried out before his 2024 London Marathon breakthrough and ditto for the Paris Olympic build up where he placed a superb 4th.

Gavin describes how very hands on the coach's presence usually is on a day-by-day basis in the Canova set up, to the extent of driving along the entirety of the route to accompany long runs. Given the altitude of over 2000m/7000 feet, the less-than-world's-fastest underfoot surface and the usually undulating routes, the coaching was more about assessing the balance of relaxation versus fatigue than the cold data of pace splits. In particular he recalls the Canova preoccupation with being "tranquil". This is maybe not quite a literal use of the word in English but conveys something like a fully controlled and relaxed state whilst working hard.

The current running world preoccupation with marathons tends to mean that elite marathoners gain higher profiles than their endurance track counterparts but neither Canova nor Gavin have any particular focus on the legendary 26.2 miles. And so the crew of runners they looked after covered the range from 3k to marathon and included a couple of 3000 metres steeplechasers. One in particular who Gavin cites as perhaps his best coaching achievement of his Kenyan era, Gladys Kipkemoi, who was just restarting her career after having a child and some troublesome injuries, yet from this constrained start Gavin helped her secure a Kenyan berth at the 2013 World Championships.

Gavin's role evolved to a paid coaching position with the Global Management team for whom Canova worked, perhaps the world leader in athlete management if measured by its leading athletes. At the same time his wife was leading on logistics at the training camp used periodically by GB and other overseas distance squads, both Federation and other high performance groups, so they upgraded early on from the tent residency.

The set up lasted four years. In a superficially bizarre but on paper at least, logical next move, Gavin took on the Chinese Federation role as women's marathon squad coach. In 2014 the Chinese political links with the UK were somewhat less strained than currently and the role had just been vacated by Canova himself who was keen to have a quality assured successor; whilst Gavin himself had wanted his next role to have a Federation backing. In practice the role proved much less fulfilling than the build up had suggested and within months he had returned to the UK. All before hitting 30 years of age.

There followed an elite-focused online and in person coaching phase all done alongside building up his Kenya Running trips company further capitalises on the knowledge and connections he developed in the country. Notable coachees in the UK included Channel Islander Lee Merrien who had previously run in the Olympic Games, World and European Championships, and John Beattie who has gained an unusual but extremely impressive UK 'record' of the longest number of years in which he has broken 30 minutes for 10k, heading towards 20 years at time of writing! It's a wonderful sequence and has had more than one coach's input including Beattie himself. Over time the business took over from the coaching so when we caught up in spring 2024 his coaching cohort had become just one runner. Gavin's is such an unusual coaching history but because it's the only one he himself has lived through he describes it as if it's fairly standard. He's still the only UK coach who has relocated lock stock and barrel to coach only Kenyan runners in their homeland.

David Turner – The Academic Enabler

In 2016 David Turner, a sports academic at Hertfordshire University, contacted me as a potential subject for his PhD on performance coaching. We'd initially crossed paths at the Herts Coaching Week at the University's fine Hatfield campus (scrimpingly narrow parking bays though, in case that last sentence has already prompted you to visit with an SUV) where he'd delivered some stirring thoughtful seminars. The project would involve me in the potentially navel-gazing task of a series of meetings with David where the subject was my coaching. So, yes, talking about myself, on an on, to someone who was professionally obliged to listen to me, even if someone really charismatic carrying a tray of canapes and chilled Bollinger appeared just behind my left shoulder.

David T was excellent to talk to and had forged a lively and evolving role in sports academia. It was a world where the word 'pedagogy' was standard fare.

David was delving into the traits that occur in coaches at performance level. I picked him up on what he intended to imply with the words "high performing coaches " as I'd recoil from any coach who described themselves that way. And he certainly delved, and so you can you as his e-doorstop of a 351-page thesis is available online. The catchy headline title is "Surfing the Turbulence" which by rights could be an unearthed Beach Boys album or a Cornish surfboard store with some dope under the counter. In fact, it has its roots in Zen ideas of the late 1960s (so not a million miles from Beach Boys territory, nor indeed light usage of narcotics). The fuller title is more elaborate and hints at the depth of intellectual thought that unfolds through the thesis "Fluctuations in self-perceptions of expertise in the long-term developmental journeys of expert-like male sports coaches".

His Doctoral thesis opens with a fine array of wisdom that wraps up one of the true innovators of middle-distance coaching, with one of the leading human beings of the last century and one of literature's greatest voices, so he is setting the bar very high from the outset. "You only ever grow as a human being if you are outside of your comfort zone." - Percy Cerutty (quoted by Herb Elliott, in The Sports Factor, 2008). "It was a favourite saying of Tolstoy that the moment one believes that he has reached his ideal his further progress stops and his retrogression begins." Mahatma Gandhi. He then sets out, amongst other things how the whole field of coaching has been unpacked by numerous academics across various ideas of behaviour, learning, motivation, progression. And as I found, it brings with it a hefty complexity of vocabulary in the concepts it examines.

David's purpose, to give full merit to his doctoral work, was to challenge each coach in his discussions to reflect and evaluate as we told our tale so that it became a more dynamic and rounded process than just a linear narrative of events and phases. What comes through is that the sort of person you are outside of your coaching will inevitably be reflected in, and influence how, you operate and are perceived as a coach. This sounds almost too obvious to state but when one reads that coaches are typically like this or like that, the one thing that coaches always will be is themselves. And so we all have to use whatever bits of our self can best serve what we are trying to do.

One sentence of my testimony I read back recently was my intention "to address steeplechase and race walk elements to a greater extent" and truth to tell I have had a nul points on both events now and in the last 20 years. I'm a follower of the events (and unlike many I have no doubt on the athletic validity of race walking albeit the debate about "lifting" will never go away) though have never been asked to contribute and nor ever yet met a runner to whom I'd suggest either event.

Looking at his work again, amongst other things it shows clearly that there is really no standard background of class, age, education, career, sporting prowess or any prior anything that particularly lends itself to the multiple traits that coaches have. The cliched question of whether it is art or science barely scratches the surface. David himself was a great example of just this variety and career progression and – if you want to put a societal tinge to it – a case study in social mobility though the 1960s to the 1990s. The man who was piling into complex behavioural studies and assessing how to link these into sport generally, and latterly into some sports coaches' case by individual case, came from a less obviously cerebral background and had taken a long time to find his way down the academic path. From a working-class background in Islington, (I think geographically and socially he shared a lot of common ground with the Islington described by Johnny Lydon/Rotten in his own autobiography 'No Blacks No Dogs No Irish'), he showed no huge academic prowess through his school days, and his first job was as a milkman. Then he moved towards PE teaching and then the academic side of this subject assumed greater prominence in his plans and so he gradually 'converted' and was throughout this period coaching football at a good amateur level. He was an excellent facilitator in my experience.

The irony with hindsight is that my time with him occurred at some sort of peak of reactive busyness combining day job, coaching at numerous levels, plus the England Athletics role plus parenting so whilst every session was lively from my perspective, I was somewhat scant on the prep that his study deserved. David T's writing has a lovely flow to it too and the case studies from karate, tennis and athletics throwing events are highly readable. Indeed, there are sports journalists who don't write with his skill or insight.

Gordon Surtees – A late glimpse

One of the most memorable 'performances' I've seen in coaching involved zero aerobic prowess but it lasted a full hour and so is clearly in the long endurance category in the wider sense. It was when Gordon Surtees received the Lifetime Achievement Award from the British Milers Club a couple of years before he died, in his mid-80s. I'd never previously come across him in person, mainly due to geography as he was based around Teesside in the North East of England and most of his coachees were from that part of the country. He had a great record at the highest level in the endurance sector and had held various national coaching roles.

He gave an extraordinary precise speech that tied in his coaching background, athletes he had coached, lessons he'd learned and a message of concern. The total absence of notes or pauses or any hesitations in the speech was remarkable. I'm sure that just as he worked out how best to coach others, he had his own technique to truly master the speech delivery.

The peculiar thing was, I didn't really agree with the problem area he had picked out. And to be fair, he was of the generation who do use the word problem rather than the bland neutral "issue".

He picked out British men's long-distance events very specifically. So, as he spelled out, he was clearly not referring to women's endurance at all nor to men's middle distance. It didn't make truly logical sense to me. Firstly, most of the leading UK long distance women are coached by coaches who also coach long distance men of comparable level. Secondly, several of the coaches of UK's leading middle-distance runners also coach some leading long-distance runners. This is the case whether within the UKA funded performance set up, in UK universities, USA pro teams or USA universities, the four scenarios which cover most but not all of the UK's biggest hitters.

My take is that there seems to have been a collective oversight that for various reasons the depth in international women's running still doesn't quite match the men's (decade by decade the gap narrows, such that in 2024 it is a closer correlation than it was in 2012 when the speech was delivered). You can see it in the stats without needing huge mathematical prowess and on a visual level you can see it as races unfold in that, simply and with occasional exceptions, the gaps grow bigger in the women's races.

As a recent example, in The Ten, a stacked 10,000m track race in the US in March 2024 with the express purpose of seeking Paris Olympic qualifiers, amidst several Brits setting tasty PBs the two standouts were Patrick Devers and Megan Keith. Keith stole the headlines with a superb 30.36, an automatic qualifier, vs the (very recently set) World Record of 28.54, and the recent road record of 28.48. Dever ran 27.08, 2nd on the UK ALL TIME list behind only Mo Farah yet fell 8 seconds shy of the Paris qualifier of 27.00 – in an event where the world record on either surface is 26.11 – so within a minute. It's a very binary scenario to present – Megan Keith was good enough to meet the Olympic standard, Patrick Dever was not. So he can be linked to the F word – 'failing' to qualify. But based on these performances is Dever actually a lesser 10,000 metre runner as a man than Megan Keith as a woman?

Europeanism

One coach development event that showed that useful material won't always come spoon fed was in Brighton. During the early years of the Brighton marathon, race founder Richard Nerurkar focused, amongst the event's various objectives, on building up its front end with some leading British runners. Always a tough ask with the race in the same April month as London and only 60 miles south of the capital. As part of this, he set up a coaching presentation for Luciano Gigliotti who could uniquely be promoted as the only person alive who had coached two Olympic marathon champions - the Italians Gelindo Bordin (Seoul 1988) and Stefano Baldini (Athens 2004), the latter in particular a momentous achievement as the East Africans had by then more numerously arrived at the top of the world pecking order. Gigliotti spoke no English and given that UK coaches can gain a licence without even the barest smattering of Italian, you can see the challenge. Fortunately, the well-connected Nerurkar managed to bring in UK based Italian Paolo Natali whose multilingual ability slotted in alongside his 2.18 marathon prowess; he expertly carried out the extremely tough job of simultaneous translation. It was just like being in the United Nations debating chamber though we didn't have to worry about Russia or Iran vetoing the details of the Marathon pace with float recovery session. The only time I've been at such a session; it certainly keeps your mind working.

Less Than A Coaching Hero There was one coach who whilst initially very helpful and supportive eventually become a person for me to avoid. When I mentioned this encouraging early support to one of my (unofficial) mentors at the time, they said "just be aware that [they] are very keen on the financial side ". This mentor was always precise in their choice of words so the unexpected comment resonated. When I first met the coach at a residential training weekend, with a woman I was coaching at the time, the coach looked at each of us and said "I assume you'll be wanting to share a bedroom" which we both confirmed, somewhat embarrassed, was definitely not the case. Years later I checked with the woman that my memory of this bizarre ice breaker was correct.

The next morning as we drove to the training loop the coach (who was one of the earlier adopters of paid-for coaching) said they divided the runners they coached into three categories " the elites; the serious recreational guys, 2.30 to 2.40 for the marathon; and the rest are muppets ". A couple of years later I was planning to go, with a quartet of coachees, to a warm weather week this coach organised. We had had a very good time the previous year and were looking to return. This year there was an additional coaching fee expected from all of us. I queried this on our behalf, saying that I was an experienced coach and now an ex-runner and so wasn't in the market to be coached, and the athletes were all coached individually and voluntarily by me so it seemed superfluous to charge them for something they weren't seeking. The reply was memorable "Well mate, you're the one with the flat in Malaga ". I was so gobsmacked I didn't have the presence of mind to correct them by saying that it was actually a house. I saw no way back from that and thus ended the link. Various other anecdotes have been passed to me to show that my advisor's initial comment was well founded.

Lads and Lasses

One trend is that, set aside from the commercial coaching (where for several years the male to female ratio of my coachees has stayed around 75%/25%) on the club volunteer level it has shifted almost totally. In the first two or three years at London Heathside I coached two men and about seven women. And the women did pretty well too, in the context of the club's profile and my relative novice status in coaching. Indeed, for whatever reason (if indeed there is a reason) the performances of these women were, with one notable exception, on a par with any of the women I've coached in the following 17 years.

As a team they won the UKA team championships in the London marathon and, with a mainly different quartet, won bronze medals in the tough Southern Cross-country championships (to clarify, both teams also had runners I didn't coach); one woman, almost the very first person I ever coached, ran 2.49 marathons twice and won both the Edinburgh and San Sebastian marathons. I've not yet coached another quicker female marathoner; yet if we compare with the male equivalent (about a 2.32) I must have coached close to 30, including numerous who are much faster; plus several of a higher level who never tried the marathon. There may be something of a self-fulfilling cycle here in that once you seem to be doing a decent job with either men or women, so others may be curious and seek you out; and conversely if you seem to be coaching no men or women above a certain level, then the perception and assumption becomes that this is just who you are and who you coach.

It's also at least in part related to the club environment you choose to be in. So London Heathside initially happened to have, for its size, a good posse of keen smart women in their 20s and early 30s, several of them relatively new to the sport, whereas the men's team at the time were largely aged 40 plus, had been training for many years and were well able to manage their own training and racing plans.

Serpentine, as mentioned above, had a growing gap between the relative performance level of the quicker men and women, and so a greater likelihood that my coaching aims could be better received by the guys; and more recently in Highgate the men's and women's teams largely operate as independent entities. This is not a fault or criticism in any way. At a very simple level, if you have 20-plus men running between say 28 to 32 minute 10k level, as at Highgate, they won't be sharing many harder running sessions with top club women running about 15 per cent slower.

I don't do coach by coach audits on this aspect but it's apparent to me that numerous coaches I know, men and women, have these odd trends and patterns over time I doubt that any of them have at any stage expressly sought to coach with such an uneven balance.

As part of the PhD sessions I did with Dr David Turner, he suggested that perhaps initially I was perceived as a relative newcomer coach and because women in general in the sport may be more receptive to hearing and trying external ideas in a face to face situation of how to progress, compared with men who may in general tend more to read their own training resources and be more confident in making their own decisions in isolation; and thus at that stage more women than men saw this new coach as a possibly beneficial option for them. Fast forward a few years and my coaching experience and CV had moved on, and – again stressing that these comments are speculative and generalised – the same sort of women may have been slightly intimidated by the PBs of the quickest males I had coached, and conversely a few more men might think that I might be the one to add some marginal gains to their DIY approach. Truly it puzzles me.

There is a wider context here, which is that in the last twenty years the number of women who have pushed ahead into the higher levels of coaching has grown significantly. But starting from a low point, the male/female split of coaches is still notably male-dominated. There are many women runners who would be unlikely to choose a male coach. Just as there are women runners who may prefer a male coach.

So I recently put this conundrum out to the women I currently coach. One response came from a 2.54 marathon runner in her early 30s who is a long-haul airline pilot – the pilot industry has just 5% females in this role. In so many words, others responded in very similar vein to her comments. *"I would rather choose a coach who is well-educated in/smart about the art of running, coaching and its physiological effects regardless of gender. I think men and women can be equally clued-up (and not!) about the specifics of women's biology and how they respond to training. I don't necessarily feel more or less comfortable working with a man or woman, more important for me is their knowledge, application thereof, and supportiveness/ empathy. I'm happy to see a gradual increase in both the number of female runners and coaches but I think that should take nothing away from competent male coaches.*

I think my approach comes from my job in that I'm obviously still severely outnumbered, so for me, whilst I have a keen interest in encouraging more women to be pilots, on a day-to-day basis, I like to think that we are 'judged' on our ability rather than on our gender!".

Another thoughtful analysis came from Kate, 30 years old and a 91 minute half marathoner. She has a mighty impressive CV and so it's not surprising that she raises some thought-provoking points.

"When I was looking for a coach, I didn't give much weight to the coach's gender. Experience, fees, and principles & process for coaching were much more important to me. There have been times when I have wondered if I should have placed a greater emphasis on the coach's gender. Usually, this

doubt emerges at the times when I feel my body is at odds with my brain and the running goals I'm going after. At these times, I wonder, if I had a female coach, would she - as someone who has the experience of being female and training with a female body - be better able to help me identify why I feel slow and incapable, and how to adapt my training accordingly? Would she be able to answer questions like, "How much do my menstrual cycle, hormonal fluctuations and birth control choices matter to my performance, in addition to other body-related variables like sleep and stress?

I suspect female coaches are probably more likely to proactively raise and engage with some of these kinds of female body-related questions that I think about but hesitate to ask my male coach. However, there's no reason a non-female coach shouldn't be knowledgeable and proactively engage on these topics... and no guarantee that a female coach would.

Overall, I think having a male coach -- especially one who's open to, or at least tolerates, these kinds of discussions -- has pushed me to think about being a female runner (as opposed to just a runner) and more broadly, female in a world where the female body is often stigmatized. But I will say... I definitely feel uncomfortable thinking and talking about this. I think it's because when I talk about being female, it feels like I'm asking for special accommodations. Frankly, I hate this: it's like I'm asking for help for a problem that no one wants to acknowledge, and that problem is my female body – something I have very little control over but impacts my every move. I strongly believe being a woman (or whatever gender) shouldn't be a problem. But I also don't think I would be helping myself or women more generally by pretending there's no difference in our bodies and experiences. My body is literally supposed to bleed once a month, every month, for decades!

So I guess I wish my male coach would proactively acknowledge these differences as part of the overall training program; one thing that comes to mind is that in the initial screening, it would be worth asking female runners, "Do you have regular periods?" And for me it would be reassuring to work with someone who has a view based in science on whether and how to adapt training based on menstrual cycles, and what kinds of birth control are best for runners."

Another runner, a senior teacher and Exam Board officer, in her 50s, fed back comments which remind us that just because something may be a trend in general, numerous individuals will not conform to that trend. She explains *"I struggled to come up with a reason WHY I chose a male coach. I came to the conclusion that …. the question needed to be rephrased as why I WOULDN'T choose a male coach. In short, gender wasn't a consideration for me at all. What did matter was the individual and whether we would get on and build a positive coaching relationship. Interestingly, having only had a female coach previously, the subject of the menstrual cycle and its impact on running performance was never mentioned until you raised it after a disastrous 5k! Now I'm at the other end of the spectrum and dealing with perimenopause and potential effects on health and exercise, I'm glad you raised hormones as I may not have considered other effects at all. Having attended an all-girls school, there was never any question that our sex would determine or influence our life path. In fact, the concept was never even entertained. It was only when I went to university that I became aware of the dynamic at play and societal responses. Having worked in education all my life (where many women are employed as teachers and middle/senior leaders), I have been immune to some of the more patriarchal structures that seem to pervade so much of life. I have become more conscious of it as I get older."*

I was curious to look at the drop off in women progressing (using typical measurable indicators of progression) through the more advanced levels of coaching.

A real eye-opener from a 2021 UK Athletics report was that in the previous decade the gender split of coaches operating at senior international championships level was men 207/women zero. (I have a caveat on this zero figure, in that at every World and European cross country championship in this period the women's Team Manager was a woman and the role would be shown in the team briefing as Team Manager/ Coach, because to the extent that the individual coach may not be present at the event, the TM would fulfil a coaching role). It seems astonishing that a whole decade passed without this apparently total absence being flagge d up. At under 20 international level (which almost everyone in the wider sport would still call elite) the number was 90 men and 23 women. Bear in mind that it typically may take a decade to progress from induction to coaching junior international so at any snapshot date you are looking at a cohort who may on average represent the coaching inductees of a decade earlier. Interestingly the junior international female coach cohort at 21 per cent slightly exceeded the number of women qualified to level 3, at 18 per cent and the highest level 4 at 11 per cent. One interpretation is that in selecting coaches for junior international teams, women seemed to be able to make a more favourable impression than their official licence indicated. Yet apparently not one of these 23 went up to the next stage.

Looking at some of the niche research on this it struck me that most of the issues mentioned could just as well have substituted "life" or "society" or "the workplace " for "performance sports coaching ". That's not to belittle either the studies or the issues but simply to make the point that my curiosity was and is whether any specific aspects about performance coaching in athletics serve to restrict women pursuing this, in a different way from how they may affect men. I'm not best placed to assess this as the women endurance coaches I know will invariably be those who have "crossed the barrier".

Purely on observation and hypothetically (it's not mentioned in the leading notes on the studies I looked at), I wonder if, as one's coaching demands build up, these can steer the coach to an unbalanced lifestyle of juggling work, family, coaching and other leisure options. It's not necessarily the number of hours of coaching itself (though it can be just that) but the drip feeding of coaching comms and demands and expectations throughout the day and indeed the evening. So the balance of fitting in coaching amidst other demands can become reversed such that the coach is, or may be perceived by those closest to them, fitting in other demands around the continual coaching commitments.

Generalizing and emphasising that there are many exceptions, coaches are often building up their coaching when they have young children and may be commuting to work and still sneaking in a daily slot for their own training/fitness. I theorise that some women coaches will foresee this scenario, the various risks it brings and decide either not to do it or to strategically defer for a few years until they have more breathing space in daily life. Typically I'd expect that more men would metaphorically beat their chest (well, maybe literally if they coach sprints) and push on at all costs, with a possible unravelling further down the road.

Coaches At Risk

This episode provided the most chilling moment of my coaching career. The epicentre of this moment lasted maybe fifteen seconds. To explain, I had for one academic year a coaching role at a 6th form college near London. It had a tidy and well-structured athlete performance academy programme for around fifteen athletes aged 16 to 18. The college funded about 3/4 of the programme costs with parents topping up the other 1/4, a few hundred pounds. I worked with a quartet of lads in the endurance events, 1500 and 3000 metres mainly plus cross country. All were good county to borderline national standard. The one who seemed most diligent and well organised was not from the local area. I'd heard that in his shared lodgings his housemates but not him had noticed various items going randomly missing. The college year ended and then around late August I received a call from the programme manager.

He named the athlete and said *"He's not returning this year. He's made some statements about you that I have to put to you. He says these are why he's not returning "*. I could almost literally feel my heart fall through the floor. I quickly cast my mind back. We had spent precisely ten minutes in a one-to-one situation when I had collected him one very rainy morning from his lodgings and driven to the county cross country championship on the other side of the town. He had turned 18 prior so nothing untoward in that.

"What has he said? " I asked.

"He says that you said he should get some drugs that would help him run faster". I almost laughed with massive relief that the "only" accusation was of suggesting he cheat by taking drugs.

I knew of course that this would immediately be proved false. I replied *"Firstly this is totally false. Which drugs did he say I offered?"*

"He couldn't remember the name".

"And where was he going to get the drugs from?"

"He said that you told him he could get them from a chemist"

It turned out that on further enquiry the real reason why he wasn't returning was that his family were unable to provide their modest share of the programme funding. It was a painful episode.

The person stayed in the sport and performed at good club level. It's a terrible thing to create lies that could potentially destroy a person's career and reputation in the sport and more widely.

The frequency with which athletic coaches are committed of offences - crimes, let's be clear- against their coached athletes is still in my view worryingly high. The sort of case you might think could occur every 5 years seems to happen at least once per year. One club in the London area with which I had numerous dealings had two of its senior coaches in prison at the same time for sexual offences against minor boys. Both had been career-long teachers and had coached to international level. I found about one of these when I emailed a colleague and asked him if we could engage him as track referee for a forthcoming meeting (he was an experienced official). The reply came "*He's serving a 5-year sentence so unlikely to be available*".

The Athletes - Coaching Some Great People (who also run fast)

Flattering Not To Deceive

One feature of coaching runners who are much quicker than you have achieved in your own sauntering is the need to mentally park quite how fast they are racing if it is faster than you can conceive. Otherwise you just end up gawping and fawning, which doesn't add to athlete performance and makes you look like a dullard. This "upper limit" is of course subjective but I've had a few coachees whose best running is slightly beyond my mental scale. So at the outset I'll fawn just the once and say that I appreciate and am in awe at how fast they race. I'm then curious to delve into quite what they see as their uppermost goals and what sort of timeframe they currently foresee for their time in the sport at their top level. Clearly there are no correct answers here but the coach and the runner have to share the goals or there's a lack of mutual belief. So for example when Alex Lepretre and I first chatted in detail he had PBs of 28.56 (which won him the England 10k champion on the road) 63.32 at half marathon when running for England in Copenhagen but no serious marathon time (he and

I didn't count his bygone 3.07 before he took things more committedly. Though the 3.07 features oddly frequently in Highgate banter). He had had about four years of training very extensively within the Highgate framework and 100 miles per week was fairly standard fare for much of the year. We didn't see Olympic selection at any event as a feasible goal, and so, looking beyond the Team England vests he had already earned at 10k and HM, we looked at the option of GB selection at either Half or Full marathon at the European championships. The minutiae vary within both the European federation and UK athletics. It's not a be all and end all that he achieves the GB vest but it certainly helps to keep the motivational fires burning beyond a less sharpened aim to simply keep doing more of the same. I'm not sure whether he or I was more deflated when the qualifying time for the European Half Marathon championship in Rome in June 2024 was set by the European federation at 61.40 or a sub 2.11 marathon.

These athlete profiles, are ordered chronologically in the order in which we first started a coaching link, which have all been done on a volunteer basis.

Will Green

In autumn 2009 I received a very thorough email from newish Serpentine runner Will Green who was in a mood of medium to high dudgeon after a relatively disappointing New York City marathon when he had clocked 2.48 when chasing 2.40 on the hilly course, "worth" about three minutes slower than a Berlin or London course, at this level.

He was then 35 years old and returning after a very long absence, having been a national level runner in his mid teens. He had run 8.53 for 3000m aged 15, and an equally impressive 1.57 for 800m at age 14 – both of which gained him entry to the English Schools Championships representing Cheshire, and had great memories of being part of the Wirral quartet who won the Youths Under 17s Northern cross country team race, in which he had placed 12th. He was injured at age 16 so spent two years out of the sport with two bouts of surgery on his shin and trapped nerve around the top of the fibula.

After school he had read Law at Leeds University at a time when it had a very strong endurance squad but Will by his own admission was building up the volume with pints of beer rather than aerobic miles. "*By the time I got to Leeds I had largely fallen out of running and it didn't take much for me to completely fall out of that lifestyle... I am not sure it was poorly diagnosed, if I am honest, I probably didn't deal with it well. I don't know how I ended up having surgery the second time.*" He left the sport, moved to London and for some 20 years had a successful career as a commodities lawyer with one of the world's leading investment banks. He seemed to succeed just by being very clever and likeable rather than any overt ambition.

When we linked up he had a four to five year plan aiming for close to a 2.20 marathon in his very late 30s and commensurate goals from 5k to half marathon. As it turned out, his peak era took a few more years to arrive but was, age for age, even more impressive. Will's day job and early bird nature (bedtime was typically 9.30pm so the London club scene was for him totally the athletic rather than the night option) meant he did all his weekday training early a.m., and had to be trained, showered, and breakfasted by 8.15.

He piled in the miles and sessions and managed a 2.28 marathon amidst other good results. Such was his commitment that one October just before he turned 40 he sent me a detailed six months plan for the next London marathon in which the average weekly volume was 102. He had not been short of occasional injuries so I commented that 26 weeks at that volume and with almost zero down weeks just had to be reined back. His running motivation was highlighted when he showed great annoyance at being sent on a work trip to Sydney for a week. The last recorded case of someone being so disgruntled at having a free trip to Australia was when young Billie Joe McAlister was sent on the final convicts' ship in 1868 as punishment for stealing a rock cake, and he faced more arduous difficulties than being jet lagged for a hefty threshold session.

As it happened, he had a very badly injury hit two-plus years (Will, not the Victorian bakery thief) and at the very lowest point, when not actually running whilst cycling through the rehabbing, suffered an apparently freak stress fracture to the sacrum "related to an absurdly low vitamin D level having spent hours indoors rehabbing and studying!" which meant in effect that the rehab timeline for the primary injury seamlessly segued into that of the subsequent injury. Though "seamless" wasn't the main descriptive word he used when the stress fracture was identified.

But eventually his patience and drive and indeed innate talent were rewarded with some superb performances as he hit age 44 and 45, all of which placed well within the Top Five ever for UK runners of his age, including one, at 5000m, which was the fastest ever for a 44-year-old or over. (It has since been surpassed by two athletes). In addition to a swathe of Southern and National team medals with the Serpentine big guns on road and cross country, individual standouts were the 14.35 5000, 30.30 for 10k just after turning 45 (his early December birthday falling neatly just ahead of the speedy Telford 10k), a half marathon 67.13 aged 45, and two 2.24 marathons at age 44 and 45, plus a truly memorable win in one of the celebrated Highgate Night of the 10000s where he scored a 30.50 PB running the last 4k solo. Perhaps his standout marathon was actually not his fastest. In the famously hot London marathon in 2018, aged 43, when temperatures at the start were a sultry 21c, rising to 23c at the finish, he was one of very few runners to set a PB, indeed many fell far short of aspirations. Running a then best of 2.27.02 he placed 11th British runner – showing a fine combination of smart pace and fighting through mounting discomfort. The large majority of runners had set their hearts on a particular goal time, which may have made great sense on a milder day, but few made adjustments for the warm day, with inevitable results.

His training was interesting on a couple of counts, and I'll stress here that in his peak years I was really just a secondary source of training input as Will drew up his own plans and I offered my tuppeny worth. Firstly, in all his faster sessions he had modulated his "recovery " to 400 metres in 90 seconds which you'll spot is hugely faster than jogging pace let alone walking. Also he did very little running indeed at anything faster than his 5000m race pace, and not that much at 5000 pace. The coaching point here is that 5000m is a long endurance event (officially it's the shortest of the long endurance events) and thus the training needs to focus very much on what the runner can handle for the first 11.5 laps before worrying about marginal gains in the last minute of anaerobic discomfort. So Will's stellar 5000m was done with virtually no pace variation lap by lap beyond a couple of tenths. One paced if you like, but most would be delighted to be so one paced.

Throughout this purple patch his hard sessions were really long and hard and even more so once you factor in the 400 metres 90 seconds "recoveries". I certainly wonder if he'd have achieved quite these outstanding later career highlights if I'd continued offering chapter and verse on the training; his big sessions were about 10 per cent heftier than what I'd consider the top end of doable; not just here and there but consistently. This is consistent with anecdotal feedback I occasionally picked up from runners who had spent several miles of a race in keen competitive battle with Will, and they described how he seemed to hit a high level of discomfort which they thought might lead to him slipping off pace, but he just wouldn't relent and it was usually they who had to let him drift away.

A little more on the human side, in addition to the statistics, brings out why Will is so impressive beyond what his PBs show. His second running career coincided with a major career change in which he left banking and retrained, starting from scratch, including a mandatory biology A level, as an osteopath. This took several years all told and included a move from North London to a small coastal town near Brighton.

At time of writing Will is 49 and, with a tricky combination of work hours plus some hefty commuting he has returned to potentially good racing form. There's been the mental requirement of accepting that the PBs aren't now attainable but there's every prospect he pulls out some more outstanding results when he is a fresher in the V50 category.

Jake Shelley

Jake was only the second under 20 I coached. One reason is that I was in a club environment with almost no juniors for some years. Primarily though it was more a matter of choice in that I had always been aware of the huge dropout rate in young age groups and knew how crushingly disappointed I'd be if someone I'd been coaching as a volunteer gave up the sport. Partly and simplistically, I'd see it as a big waste of all my time and commitment. Notwithstanding that the athlete may have enjoyed the experience and valued the input for however long it had been provided. I decided that as a volunteer I'd only coach those who had passed through the main causes of dropping out including starting at university.

And so I first met Jake at a coaching day I was hosting with Stella Bandu when he was year 13 at school and had just won the Middlesex schools senior cross country champs and had a good national profile via Shaftesbury Barnet. I'd actually seen him online when he took the username Jake Shelley on a running forum and then introduced himself as "Hi my name is Jake Shelley " which belied what a sharp mind he has. To be fair he was only Year 12 then and was just seeking a running partner whilst he did a recce of Birmingham University. About 18 months later he was at Oxford University. He studied the same subject at the same college as Margaret Thatcher though so far he's done nothing to drive deep divisions and resentment across swathes of British society. But hey, never say never.

He was known as a very investigative student of the sport with a stack of knowledge and ideas to match his high ability. When we started the coaching link, he mentioned as an afterthought that in his early years he had dabbled with cycle racing and had won the national hill climbing champs in his age group. It struck me that only a very talented athlete would have been national champion and leave it as a footnote on the aerobic CV. He was very candid about the stresses of his coursework demands with hours of experiments and reports (some other subjects may offer a more runner-friendly lifestyle). He was part of a cohort that even by Dark Blues standards was particularly gifted; undergrad teammates included his long term friend Luke Caldwell who went on to have great success from 5000 up to a 2.11 marathon debut, Andrew Heyes who became a GB international over the same range of events, and the equally talented Tom Frith who had a slightly less seamless pathway and who spans the performances from a 49 second 400 metres at school to a 2.18 marathon. All except Frith did postgraduate athletics scholarships at USA endurance hubs in New Mexico and Oklahoma.

Over the years Jake was coached by himself (the longest serving coach by duration!), myself, Alan Storey, Joe Franklin in New Mexico and Carlos Handler, during a post Masters stint at altitude. And here's the thing, one way or another Jake's best performances under each "regime" were very much of a level, give or take very little, as each other. This sort of scenario is in my experience not unusual. In Jake's case the variables have also varied over the period. He had many months of altitude during his New Mexico days, which hasn't been replicated. He had almost daily contact with a coach in New Mexico, and then he didn't. And his post 2019 road results are with the new breed of shoes which are about 1 to 2% faster than their footwear forebears. And he now has a full-time job which however flexible it may be surely doesn't have quite the flex of being a PhD student. So currently at age 33 with a full-time job in Switzerland self-coached Jake has recently run 14.03 for a 5k road race. His career best of 13.46 (sea level) was whilst training at altitude as a part time Master's student under coaching legend Joe Franklin at New Mexico. His 3000 PB of 7.59 was with my input whilst his best winning race performance (note that athletes of this level actually don't win the large majority of their races!) was via Alan Storey.

Jake has remained a lifelong member of Shaftesbury Barnet which, whilst it has seen several of its junior prodigies not stay in the sport for the long haul as seniors, has a remarkably good record of very rarely having its leading members transfer to other clubs. He had good luck in his home location as a youngster being about a one-mile warm up jog from Copthall track, having lots of fields and trails on the rural edges of Mill Hill and Totteridge almost on the doorstep whilst being about three minutes drive from the M1 to access no end of national racing locations. From a family who major on creative artistic careers Jake followed a scientific path and has moved though the ranks of the international anti-doping agency. At the Paris Olympics he had the sport specific manager role for testing in cycling. It's the only sport in which a team's doping system has won a literary award, courtesy of Tyler Hamilton.

Historically, and simplifying over 15 years of high level training and racing, Jake has kept on relatively low mileage for his level, mainly to reduce foot injuries to which he has been vulnerable; has always done a large proportion of his training off road and pavement; and has a nice knack of putting a load of fast intervals together in a race compared to the recovery he needs to carry out the same pace in training sessions.

It was interesting to catch up with Jake, now based in Geneva long term, to draft this piece and he commented " it does make me reflect on 'what might have been'. I remember that you once told me that you thought I could run what was then the 'normal' championship qualifying time for 5000m of ~13:25, and it does frustrate me that I haven't done that, because I also think I might have been able to get close."

Since his track racing peak, the Qualifying Times at elite championships 5000s have come down by between 1 and 2 seconds per lap. Whilst that is not a vast step change, and in the context of the new shoe template 'neutralising' at least a small part of this, it does make a real difference into where a posse of elite runners, men and women, now 'fit' and, maybe, just tilts the scales further from them staying in the sport when they are past university (or even before). Admittedly one is bandying around hypothetical numbers here but even in my one current club I could pick out two or three runners who 15 years ago, all things being equal might have been in a with a long-term shout at qualifying for a big championship at the longer distances. Now, when the minimum qualifying standards are almost in line with the fastest ever by a UK-born athlete, the pool of likely candidates is surely very much tinier.

As a lot of Jake's training has been done solo down recent years, he has been a regular user of the Easy Interval training method developed very effectively by Dutch innovator Klass Lok. It's something I delved into and in an ideal world would have liked to apply more widely. The ideal world though is a little separate from almost all club endurance group sessions and the spread of ability within almost every club group which makes it harder to do EIM sessions as a close-knit group. I've described it in more detail below as it seems to me a slightly outlying system.

Martin O'Connell – The Mileage Munching Professor
On a late autumn evening I took a phone call from a well-spoken

young woman who described how her boyfriend did some running and seemed to be "quite good at it". I asked her for a little bit of background and teased out he'd done a 2.53 marathon and trained quite regularly but with no great structure or purpose. She bought him a coaching meeting with me for a Christmas present (ridiculous sentence to write, but that's what happened). Some thirteen years later I wonder with hindsight if he could have easily and happily remained a 2.53 guy with some superb socks and truly deluxe after shave. As it turned out, his girlfriend's (now wife) "quite good" was a very sensible summary. The runner in question was highly academic and modestly balanced his career prowess, in which he initially worked as an economist for around a decade with the Institute for Fiscal Studies (one in 400 applicants secures a job there) with great training commitment. To cut a long story short, Martin gradually and in a non-linear way progressed, as part of the strong Serpentine squad, to a 2.22 marathon in Houston in January 2024. This left him top of the UK annual rankings for four weeks, until precisely 10.39 on the morning of the Seville Marathon when a few Brits, who'd headed out with the 8.30 starting gun, started to pile in and displace him several notches further down. It's the sort of time which now slots in on the cusp of the UK Top 50 in a given year, and about 6th to 8th amongst his Scottish compatriots. His previous PB was a 2.25 in Indianapolis where the wind speed was so ferocious that the race weather merited its own discussion thread on letrun.com. He had numerous bumps along the way to his peak so far, including covid lockdowns (not unique there of course).

He now works around an austere sounding training regime in Madison, Wisconsin where in his mid-30s he took up a prestigious Assistant Professor post in Economics at that State's University. An odd feature of his set up is that this university has a fantastic squad of endurance athletes on scholarships – often including a Brit or two - training right on his doorstep but he's not been permitted to do any running with them. This is the school's policy, to be clear, he hasn't been personally banned. Thus he ploughs a very solitary furrow on road and treadmill and fits in his heaviest 90-95 mile weeks around his professorial demands. As one would expect and hope, the coaching input evolved and became eventually very much light touch. Now so light that he could reasonably be described as self-coached. The only time I've heard him swear was when after setting a big 10k PB at the Leeds Abbey Dash the race organisers belatedly announced that all times on that day were invalid because the course had been found to be some 23 metres short of the exact 10k required. Officially, the "distance has been re-assessed after the event and due to slight alterations in the course landscape… " which seemed rather evasive on organisational accountabiliry. Martin found a shorter word to convey his frustration.

One thing we maybe take for granted in the UK is the number and accessibility of good level races year-round and pretty much across the country. In the USA it's very different. They do have tremendous national depth at top level but it is spread across a huge area, has an almost separate professional and university (National Collegiate Athletics Association) system; and whilst any clued up Brit can name a series of the best USA races, there are 51 states and 52 weeks to cover. In short, outside of the handful of megacities, serious racing is a financially and logistically much bigger demand than in the UK and the bigger European nations. So he now categorises a race as accessible if it needs only one air flight to get there.

Chris Wright - Talented Socialite Takes Extended Hiatus

Chris was the type of runner who I would never imagine joining Serpentine. In theory his previous running CV showed him as someone who picked up the nuanced differences between the old and new style clubs and was too established an athlete to seek out the latter. He had come through the classic club system in the young athletes' categories and had shown quite some talent. He had placed 13th and 19th in the English Schools cross country champs (as a Cambridgeshire rep, he ran for Nene Valley Harriers) – positions just shy of the team that is chosen by England for the Home Countries schools international, and indeed the sort of level that can have American university scouts dangling athletic scholarship offers. He moved on to Leeds Metropolitan University within that city's leading endurance network. Moving to London and initially pitching up south of the river he soon moved north, and he was at, for him, a rather moderate fitness level when he joined Serpentine and soon made a mark both socially and athletically. He approached me in early 2017 and I was very flattered on three counts; he was clearly a talented runner, was a very affable and articulate guy, and I knew that he had previously been very well coached by Russ Prosser and Graham Williams at club level and the renowned Andy Henderson at Leeds. He mentioned sessions such as 24 x 400 metres with short recoveries so I thought we would share some endurance training values. Simply because he was talented and some way off his peak it was no great coaching test to support him through fairly swift progress. These abilities meant we considered what he might achieve in the longer term; what he was willing to commit to the sport; and for how long (he was still only 25 at this stage). By coincidence I thought his ceiling in performance might be very similar to what might be achievable, in the women's events, by Izzy profiled below. Along the lines of sub 14 minutes/sub 29 minutes/63 minutes for 5k/10k/Half marathon respectively (each of which is about 10 seconds per mile faster than his actual PBs). The sort of times that 99.9% of runners would bite your hand off to achieve. But not times that change your status as an 'amateur' runner. Clearly numerous runners do assess that this level is a very exciting thing to achieve, as the national rankings show, just below the very peak of the pyramid.

At that stage we left the marathon hanging unspoken - he had too much left to achieve further down the distances, and at that stage his mileage was too low to make a marathon transition sensible.

Given that his historic mileage was on the low side for the level he had reached, almost every race showed some progression from the previous one – that's the 'high aerobic responder' trait. He had gradually built to average maybe 55 miles per week at this stage so had plenty of upside. He had a great running efficiency, developed and embedded in his younger training years – when fit, he could be doing 400 metres laps of 69/70 seconds and appear to have plenty of spare gears in hand. This continued through to the early months of 2019 with arguably his best run of all being the Inter Counties cross country where over 12k he was barely a minute behind men who earned GB selection for the world championships in this trial race.

One memorable race – which I watched remotely on a live stream, this is just what summer Saturday nights were invented for - was his PB 5000 of 14.29, set in the British Milers Club B Race at Loughborough. Not on the surface the most fascinating event – after all, how amazing can a B race be? – but the very even level of the large majority of the field mean that as they hit the home straight with just 500 metres left there were still almost 20 guys sticking together in the leading group with each one of them thinking that they might end up anywhere between 1st and about 18th, with 90 per cent of the race completed; very unusual at this level.

To simplify the position as it evolved, Chris (having been a few months ahead of his coach in transferring to Highgate) eventually decided that the level of training he'd need to commit to in order to reach his full potential, and what fulfilment that potential would add to his enjoyment of the sport thus far, was not a favourable equation and he largely stepped off the gas. He has used the specific word 'hiatus' on his current situation rather than retirement or departure and so he has, for a while, time on his side should a grand sustained return become desirable. One benefit that Serpentine provided for him that far outstrips a few team medals and fancy PBs is that he linked up with his partner and mother of his young daughter, so that is a classic example of the famed Serpie social side operating successfully. Athletically, he ran the 2024 Manchester Marathon in 2.37. Nothing remarkable there but in 2023 his late Autumn parkruns were no quicker than what in April became his Marathon Pace. And like all his previous achievements, an outlying conversion of training volume to result. I think the sport misses out by not having him in it.

Izzy Clark – Unfulfilled Talent

The most disappointing case of my entire coaching time, by some margin, has been that of Izzy. In this light I'm very grateful she's willing to be dissected here. In terms of the gap between what she could have, in my view, achieved, and what she managed, it is a large shortfall and she is almost literally the last person who could deserve the very bad luck she incurred, to the extent that her time in the sport, as a sport rather than a fitness habit, was maybe four years of which less than half was performing unhindered.

She had long been a casual runner with a school and club hockey background. About 18 months before we met, in 2017, she had set herself a sub 40 minutes 10k goal. This proved somewhat conservative and so when we crossed paths, shortly after she'd joined Serpentine, she had recently nipped under 35 minutes in a certified race being just pipped by a woman who had previously run at 10,000 metres for Great Britain. In summary, she was running mostly about 80 kms per week or a tad more, with very little precise structure but still some reasonable variety of paces and distances.

She was an extremely modest person, not bothered by 'missing out' on drinking or social excess, and whilst she had read some bits and pieces about the sport she was not steeped in science. In fact, she had a degree in history from Oxford and her working life had been spent mainly in charities working for women's rights in the developing world. So, you can see that she prioritised social change and justice over monetising her ability. After we chatted, she confirmed her commitment to maximising her ability at 5k to half marathon and I was pleased that she made no mention of the full marathon. For the first and only time in all my coaching years I went for full proactive pushiness and said that I thought she should be coached and that I should be the one to coach her unless she would rather not. I suggested she could aim to run for GB at something like the European Cup 10,000 on the track (at the time, this event had a three-year agreement between the UK and European Federations to host the races at Parliament Hill) or the World Half Marathon champs, the relatively "low hanging fruit" for Team GB compared to the Olympics or World track races. I was convinced these GB goals were realistic if things went well over three to five years (she was 31 at the time).

One way or another, things never flourished the way that seemed possible and the odd thing amidst this great disappointment is that there was no obvious cause for the shortfall from either her or my perspective. The two things which seemed to crop up were little injuries out of the blue which possibly had roots in her hypermobility (which various physios noted when they treated her) and some erratic sleep cycles that likely left her under recovered and vulnerable in an unspecified way. She even had a long phone consultation with one of the leading UKA doctors to whom we gave extensive briefing notes. She never particularly raised the training volume beyond about 85 to 90 kms per week, which was nothing truly hefty for her level and the loading was nothing unusual over any given week or fortnight. Her career bests stalled at 34.29 for 10000m and 76.04 (all set before the new faster shoes were available). Over the covid period in 2020-21 some of her best ever long efforts in training sessions suggested she was in substantial PB shape but then out of the blue, a day or two after a session had gone excitingly well with no worries during or immediately after, a physical problem, often in or around the lower back, would flare up.

In spring 2022 we last spoke and it was a sadly memorable conversation in which Izzy decided that after all these setbacks and literal discomfort she had finally lost the motivation to try a further comeback with whatever physical rehab might be available. So her racing days were over. Catching up with her recently, and having confirmed that her extremely low online presence had remained as elusive as it had previously been, I was pleased and relieved that she has established something not unlike the free flowing "as you like it" regular running habit she had before we met. Of course, my perspective is not hers so she looks back from summer 2024 and says "From my perspective, the buzz after completing your more brutal sessions, and sense of achievement in making progress - even if it didn't translate into race times- was a wonderful thing to have. I far surpassed my own expectations of what I could achieve. So I feel very lucky to have crossed paths and undoubtedly got far further, and learned more, than I would have otherwise." So as we have seen at other stages of this book, at the root it's the experience rather than the garmin data or Power of 10 listing that really matters.

I'll be surprised if I encounter this sort of athlete journey again as it seems so terribly harsh on the runner. The following may sound complacent, but I truly don't find anything that with hindsight I would have done more of or less of, or differently, either quantitatively or qualitatively.

Alex Lepretre

Alex is generally known as a relatively late starter in the sport. He did have an initial pre-teen dabble with the 1500 metres within Barnet schools, and a handy 4.47 aged 13 but at Queen Elizabeth Boys grammar school he was focused more on rugby and it was only at the back end of his university years in London where he studied Law that he resumed any structured running and as he approached his early 20s he wasn't an obvious standout. He credits the 2012 double gold medal glory of Mo Farah as being part of the inspiration to raise his own running level. Farah has often said that he aims to inspire younger runners and so here we have a case in point.

Living in Whetstone, North London he raced mainly at the local Oakhill parkrun and took about four years to break 16 minutes. 2017, aged 23 to 24, was a breakthrough season as his 3k and 5k times tumbled to 14.34 and 8.21 and the next year he changed club affiliation from Barnet and District to Highgate. He had been training with them for a while and his transfer added to what was already a national standard team. He was always keen on cross country and did very well particularly on the longer races. His PBs also continued to edge forward and in December 2022 he had a particularly memorable victory in the Telford 10k which incorporated the England 10k champs and taking his PB down below 29 minutes, which he then trimmed to 28.53 running for England in Valencia. A couple of months prior he had zipped to a 63.28 Half Marathon best in Copenhagen as part of an England team.

I started the coaching link with him just after Telford (he had previously been guided by Ben Pochee for some years) and the specific brief was to adapt to future marathon goals. The aforementioned PBs still stand though in June 2023 he scored a 5000m PB on a hot Loughborough night of 14.06, albeit slightly slower than his 13.55 on the road. He had already stacked up a few years of regular 100 miles per week and frequently a little more. Unusually, he combines this very high mileage with a fairly happy injury free history in the main, a full-time job as a commercial lawyer and, aside from regular DIY yoga, no discrete strength and conditioning. Like many a hardened mileage muncher his overview is that if he has to choose between an easy 5 or 6 miles running or spending 40 minutes on some purposeful resistance work it will always be the former that wins out. I think the opposite is worth trying though. As part of our dialogue on this he once sent me a Letsrun link which claimed world record holder and Olympic 10,000m champion Joshua Cheptegei "had never been into a gym" though I'd guess that a rural agricultural upbring in Kenya has more 'invisible' strength training than does mulling on the niceties of tort and contract law in North London. Though the rugby may well have been helpful in making him resilient for later years

The main training adaptations that he's made for the marathon are - and you've likely guessed this - in the details of the long runs at steady pace and quicker, and the mid-long sessions that hover between Half Marathon Pace and Marathon Pace. It's all there on strava and much of the pacey specific training is done at Battersea Park which is as fast a surface as you will find.

His two better marathon results thus far were both in London. A 2.15.01 debut in 2023 (or 2.14.61 as I like to record it to tease out a sub 2.15 clocking) in which he had to run an unhelpful amount of the race in isolation as he fell in no man's land between pacing groups. Then 2.15.34 in 2024 where he had good company on a slightly blustery morning. On both occasions we had thought that if everything went just right he might push into 2.13 territory. As things stand, there are possible goals for the European Championships in 2026 or if it goes ahead in its usual format the Commonwealth Games. Whilst he can do his best to achieve progress, he will then be in the hands of the European Federation's own entry criteria and then the UKA application of its own standards, or Team England at Commonwealth level.

Currently he is running at almost identical level as Jacob Allen and they are good friends and frequent training partners. Perhaps surprisingly Alex as the City lawyer has slightly more flexibility in his running versus working balance than does teacher Jacob. Of course, he has to put in the work and occasionally has awkwardly timed Court sessions (he attends online) in very different time zones such as Bermuda and Singapore. But he does the majority of his hours on a Work From Home basis (he lives in Highgate) and he is of course very disciplined in time management, which means he is able to run twice most days without heading out at the toughest hours of very early morning or deep into the evening. A very sociable chap, most of his easy runs are done with club company, sauntering mainly off road between 60 and 75 minutes, picking up and dropping off local teammates along the way at around 7 minutes per mile or a little slower. His employers understand the commitment he makes in order to run at international level and he has the flexibility to occasionally use slots of annual leave to do some of his heftiest marathon prep sessions midweek .

A couple of anecdotes reveal what sort of a character he is. Firstly he is willing to help others where he can do so. Thus, ahead of one year's Highgate Night of the 10,000 PBs someone doing a pre-event video blog wanted to interview him DURING the club's Tuesday rep session. Going the extra mile in courtesy as he always does, he gave brief snippets of chat to the interviewer and the twist here was that the session was 18 x 300m with an active rolling 100m jog in about 35 seconds so his banter was done whilst on the move and against the clock.

He is also known to like the occasional drink. Usually this is indeed just 'a drink". Though eight days before his London marathon debut in 2023 he had a friend's 30th birthday do that he felt he needed to attend. He had just run a tremendous long leg at the National 12 stage relay – his performance over the odd 5.4 miles likely on a par or better than his 10k best. I asked him what he'd had to drink and he replied " Oh, a couple of pints" and there followed a tiny pause which sounded very much like an implied full stop. So I was right on the verge of replying " No worries with 8 days to go" when the sentence continued "... and a couple of cocktails and a few shots". Then there was an actual full stop. The marathon went very well so there was in all likelihood no discernible adverse effect.

He is a highly popular guy and like Jacob he broadly expects to push on at this very demanding level for another five to six years or so but as things stand would expect to take the foot off the big mileage pedal towards his late 30s.

Jacob Allen – Thoroughbred with heart on sleeve

One of Highgate's Big Beasts (as evidenced by a clutch of club records from 10k to Half Marathon) Jacob came through the classic schools and local club route – in his case the club of Rugby and Northampton). He was a good but far from spectacular runner in his teens and the breakthrough came at around age 20 when he hacked into his PBs with 8.19 and 14.24 at 3000 and 5000 metres respectively. No doubt linked to upping the training load and quality at St Mary's University and courtesy of the coaching legend Mick Woods. The next year a further leap forward to 8.05 and 13.53 and post St Mary's he gained a one-year scholarship at San Francisco University to do his Masters. For the last 5 years he's had various phases of fine and consistent results mixed with troublesome foot injuries which can mean some ebbs and flows in motivation, but his talent – and a sensible and thoughtful approach to how to maximise it – has always stayed constant.

Jacob is a PE teacher at an Inner London comprehensive school just on the boundary of Islington and the City of London, so one of the country's most polarised areas of affluence versus its opposite, and therefore he deals with some challenged kids. Maybe linked with the inclusivity that goes with his job, or maybe just because he's a fine fellow, he is very down to earth and approachable at training and races and has just as much conversational time with much less accomplished runners as with his illustrious peers. He seems to consistently do the extra teaching mile at work and the better the results of the numerous teams he manages, the more after school matches he has to be involved in. The old impression of teachers having a relatively comfortable working life with long holidays has long been upended by the modern demands. The holidays are a trade off in that across the three terms there is no flexibility on days off and the amount of hours done outside school "opening hours" is high. So double runs are very hard to factor in and the number of days per week in term time when there is time and energy to do a long or hard (or both!) session after work is limited. So if you look at Jacob's Strava data on about five days out of seven you won't see anything particularly notable. But his fast stuff is in technical parlance "not hanging around ". I had my first proper coaching meeting with Jacob in August 2023 and literally as we met at a local pizzeria we watched his phone screen for the first 3 minutes and 30 seconds which covered the Budapest World Championships 1500 metres and the memorable win by Josh Kerr. A nice omen?

Perhaps Jacob's stand out PB at time of writing is his 47.13 for 10 miles which placed him a tremendous 2nd in Portsmouth's prestigious Great South Run. This came in October 2023 and as context it was after a heavily reduced running load over much of the early summer as he struggled to gradually overcome plantar fasciitis. So whilst he had put together several good weeks of training it was indeed weeks and not months. On the day I thought to myself that ducking just under 48 minutes would have been excellent though I didn't feel any benefit would be had by sharing this with someone of his level and experience. Just as well as I'd clearly have been suggesting an unhelpful constraint on his ability that morning!

Compared to many runners of his level he is quite open about how emotions affect his running mindset which is one part of why he is such an interesting person to liaise with. Jacob's best 5000m time, from 2018, is 13.43 and whilst everyone who knows him and the sport well is confident that he can take some margin out of this, I've not heard anyone suggest he can sneak the Olympic Qualifying Time of sub-13.05. It's a time that has some resonance too, as his friend and roommate from both his UK and USA University days, Jack Rowe, clocked 13.04.75 for the distance in his own Olympic quest. At 10,000 the scenario is similar, his recent PB of 28.44 sits against the Olympics QT of 27.00, a time just two men born in Europe have ever achieved (both with 26.59, in 2024).

So in theory he could continue to plough his energy and time and plans to focus totally on the running, whilst expecting that the progression of PBs will not substantially change his status in the sport. That is, he won't make an Olympic or Worlds track team, won't make a viable or stable living income from the sport, whilst putting big constraints on everything else that a gregarious 29-year-old might be doing with their life.

That leaves the possibility of the marathon which that 10-mile time and the relatively moderate (at this level) mileage he has so far been doing, may be something slightly less daunting. The current Olympic

Qualifying Time is 2.08.10 (with some other convoluted rankings criteria also providing an entry pathway) which is itself staggeringly tough but, simply, the biggest marathon stage of all seeks about 80 runners on the start line versus 25 for the 10000 and around 40 for the 5000 (which has two or three heats to whittle down to 15 runners for the final). Hugely difficult of course, but those variations in entry sizes make a difference. Such that nations such as Germany, Australia, France, Italy, Belgian and Spain and indeed UK can manage to gain 2 or even the maximum 3 marathon slots with native born runners whilst at 10,000 metres their respective native records don't even approach the Olympic baseline.

Even aside from this highest of benchmarks, Jacob is currently minded that the road races are what truly excites him and makes it all worthwhile. For those of us for whom a 5000m time of 13.43 seems like an amazing thing to do, we have to accept that the runner's mind is indeed theirs and, once they have partaken of a wide range of what the sport offers at high level, it's not for us to tell them which parts of it they should prefer.

His official marathon CV is one DNF in London 2024 though, paradoxical as this may sound, he ran well and sensibly on his debut, being on for a low 2.14 time when at around 34k deep cramps struck and he came out around 3k later. In training he had covered a solo 2.31 on a circuitous London route with his heart rate and perceived effort both staying impressively low. That guarantees nothing but suggests that the distance itself and the very long time on feet (this for a man with a 3.43 1500 metres in his history) is not insurmountable. A work in progress.

The reinvention of Double Threshold training?

This interlude is not to offer anything new or insightful into double threshold – which has been thoroughly picked apart elsewhere. I make the points in this section to indicate that in the modern era anything relating to running training methods that may be presented as being 'new' or 'innovative' will be less groundbreaking than it may be trumpeted as. I've picked on Double Threshold because it has picked up lots of attention and indeed additional practitioners in the last few years.

Two overarching factors are that if it leads to more runners achieving better results than that would be welcome; and that it requires two significant running efforts on the same day which immediately narrows down the number of runners who have the training background, the opportunity, and the will to do it. On reading some technical pieces on it the major takeaway for coaching purposes, in adding to whatever I already understood about it, is that training at around Anaerobic threshold pace incurs a far lesser degree of microtears (about an 80% reduction) on key muscle fibres such as those in the quadriceps (thighs) than is incurred when running at the faster speed of a runner's VO2 max. For anyone who's ever known the muscle soreness the day after an interval session at around your 3k race speed, this is quite a difference. So, again simplifying, if you can get a high aerobic stimulus but without the trade off in muscle microtears (let's call it 'fatigue' for this purpose) then it's a benefit worth having. There are of course an infinite number of efforts that can be filed under 'training at VO2 Max' and ditto as 'Training at Anaerobic Threshold' but this isn't the place to delve into them, and how they can be moulded into this protocol.

The wet behind the ears answer might be that Jakob Ingebritsen or more accurately his father and long term but now former coach Gjert pioneered this method. The smarter money might be on their Norwegian elite predecessor Marius Bakken. He was known at the time of his peak in the early 2000s to take a more scientific approach to his training than most of his rivals and peers, on his way to several long-lasting Norwegian records until the remarkable Ingebrigtsen clan got rolling a decade or so later. Bakken was considered by those who knew his training to have truly maxed his potential with his approach. But wait. Take a dip into 'How They Train: Long Distances' (1974) by Fred Wilt, and particularly the few pages allocated to Australian ground breaker Ron Clarke (coaching use aside, I just gained quite the surge of greedy satisfaction on discovering its starting price on Ebay is over £80, used, so I'll hang on to my copy. And ditto the equally highly valued 'How They Train: Middle Distances').

Back in the mid-1960s, when men at their athletic peak were still called Ron (except when they were called Derek, as in the case of his

Aussie contemporary Derek Clayton who tore up the previous marathon rankings), Clarke went on a world record rampage that culminated in world records of 13.16 at 5000 metres and 27.39 at 10,000 metres, both big margins of advance. Factor in new breed shoes and wave lights and, approaching 60 years later, these times still stand up to within about 2 per cent of what the best sea level runners anywhere can achieve. Which again undermines what all the supposed "one per centers" in recent decades are really worth.

Take this on board from Wilt's book - "Although Clarke does not run so fast in training as to exhaust himself it would be a gross error to describe his training as primarily long slow runs. On the contrary.... his training may be accurately described as consisting almost exclusively of long fast runs. On flat surfaces it is not unusual for Clarke sometimes to average faster than 5 minutes per mile for distances up to 10 miles and to approach 5 minutes per mile for distances up to 14 miles ". At this time the word "threshold " wasn't yet a thing in training parlance, though true enough the word " double " was pretty standard, if only so that your average Aussie guy knew how much beer to drink versus a normal intake. So there you have it, with his twice daily runs Clarke was pretty much hovering around his anaerobic threshold, but largely just on the "comfortable " side of it, several days per week. And the faster twitch side was covered off almost year-round with sets of 200s and 400s and Clarke also made several weekly visits to a gym. The drills he went through would be fairly standard 60 years on and in this context Clarke worked as an accountant so there was, in adulthood, no "invisible" strength training, hence the inclusion of discrete conditioning.

Of course the double threshold approach can now be finessed for those with the commitment and resources to take series of lactate readings rep by rep and session by session (as the elite Norwegians do – at around £2 per single lactate test strip, and you might use 6 to 15 strips in a session, they are perhaps the world's best placed nation to have the cash to do so). But let's not disregard that hard work, logic, experiment and experience were heading down this path decades before it even had a name. Indeed, one can credibly trace this back even further by looking at the mammoth interval sessions that the groundbreaking Czech Emil Zatopek was doing in the late 1940s and early 1950s. The sheer volume of the sessions meant that top racing speeds couldn't really be hit and so the paces per repetition were one way or another around his anaerobic threshold. This was before any sort of reliable lactate testing was done "in the field " for such athletes. It seems that a large amount of intuition, logic and trial and error was in the mix. That is, they knew they needed to practice training at around racing pace to build up relevant adaptations ("race fitness"); they knew that within reason "more was better ", whilst also recognising that an unremitting battery of volume plus intensity would break them down with injury or at least insufficient recovery; and so Zatopek refined what worked for him. And his stash of Olympic golds and world records showed that it really did work.

Chosen Words

I often ponder on what, if anything, to say to a runner just or shortly before they tackle a target race. There's the risk of overtalking and overthinking, which is very unlikely to be of benefit. There's the wish to avoid banality or cliché. There's a generic idea that anything more than three coaching tips at the same time is counterproductive, in that by adding a fourth or even fifth the coachee will likely start diluting their assimilation of the previous three. My favourite pre-race coaching tip of all time comes from sprint coach legend Joe Douglas. His protege Carl Lewis was about to head out for the 200 metres final at the 1984 Olympics at Los Angeles, so somewhat high stakes. Lewis asked Douglas for any final tips on how best to tackle the race. "Run fast, turn left " was the advice. Lewis won.

Klaas Lok's Easy Interval Method

Almost everything else I have come across in the supposed evolution of endurance running training in the last 30 years seems to be a very minor variation (if that, sometimes it is just a rebranding of something that is already established) on a theme, whereas the EIM goes a little further in stripping back the usual framework and then reallocating the components in a slightly unusual way. If you do the large majority of your training alone then this approach may be worth considering as there's no requirement to meld its details within a group environment.

The book's English version has been excellently translated by Russ Mullen, himself a fine case study of Klaas's approach. It includes photos of runners crawling backwards uphill – apparently a cruel but effective core strengthening drill, and which recalls Australian innovator Percy Cerruty's approach in using the natural environment in creative ways. The 'philosophy' will, at the very least, make you think and question why do exactly what you do, whether as coach or runner.

As an athlete, Lok had excellent credentials from his peak in the late 1970s to mid 1980s, including a 7:51 3000 metres (and 2nd place in the European Indoors), perhaps the standout on his racing CV was 20th in the World Cross Country in 1980 when the European and USA strength in depth was immense.

Interestingly he matched this grinding endurance with superb closing speed, with a swathe of Dutch championship wins – once closing a 5000m track race with a blistering 53.5 which for a man who couldn't do a one off 200m in under 25 secs is outstanding. These snippets of data illustrate that a major focus on aerobic conditioning combined with retention of relatively high speeds done without fatigue (achieved by virtue of the session design) meant that fairly light exposure to highly anaerobic stresses proved a tremendously effective balance of stimulus.

His coaching 'portfolio' was impressive, and particularly in the context that his coachees were drawn largely from a provincial pool around Utrecht and he had no official Federation role in which to 'recruit' athletes.

Women he coached attained a 5k PB of 15:22; and, a separate female coachee a 10,000m PB of 32.22, a male zipped to a 62.29 at Half marathon; plus a Veteran aged 40 scorched to an 8:15 3000; and a remarkable 55 year old Woman clocked a 79 Half Marathon.

Perhaps the most well-known case study is that of world class 800 metres runner Bram Som. Aged 26 he ran a long-lived Dutch record of 1:43.4 using a 'classic' training schedule. Three years later, after injuries so significant that his running was confined to 4 days a week, he spent a season using the EIM and clocked 1:43.5 and made the World

Championship final (where just 0.59 seconds behind the gold medal placed him 7th!).

It's hard to summarise the approach to be both thorough, accurate and concise at the same time. Simplifying, the bare bones of the EIM takes in one hard session (or a race) per week, usually of a mixed pace nature – fartlek if you will – that keeps in touch with the demands and stimulus needed for the athlete's target distance(s).

The one detailed example Lok sets out is a truly multi-faceted session and duration (for him as a 28 minute 10k athlete) was 95 to 105 mins all in, with 11 strands not counting warm up and warm down. The other days are nearly all built around the EIM which if it has one specific benefit that 'traditional' steady state training may lack is the preservation of 'reactivity'; the Dutch word is 'souplesse' and words like 'elasticity' or 'dynamism of stride' come close.

Terminology aside, the principle is that it is based on speed (using that word quite flexibly) without heavy aerobic/metabolic fatigue, so the principle of continued recovery between truly intense efforts is not compromised. The staples of EIM are the likes of 10-12 x 200m at around 3k pace with equal distance slow running recovery; and 10 x 400m at between 5k and 10k race pace with equal distance slow running recovery; and 6 to 8 x 1000m at around Half Marathon pace with equal duration easy running as recovery.

All the faster reps have a 10 second walk before starting and after completion, which further lessens the overall intensity. The book covers all standard distances from 800 metres to marathon, with the wider base of case studies between 3000 metres and Half Marathon.

It's worth mentioning that for marathon runners the author fully buys into regular (but not every week) long and very long runs, always with some sort of faster shorter efforts.

The particular advantages of the EIM over traditional methods (which he mentions in passing are often based around important and often reductive misunderstandings of relevant details of what Lydiard actually recommended) include the following:-

• Too many runners run some combination of too much one paced mileage and do too many intense interval sessions at or around VO2 max, or indeed faster and harder.

• Their fast interval sessions eventually, by a combination of being too frequently too hard become destructive rather than productive; and their easy recovery runs are detrimental to their fast twitch capacity and gradually lead to poorer running form and movement, and a poorer running economy (RE) which more than offsets the gains in RE that the mileage itself might be promoting by other physiological adaptations.

• That the best athletes in the world by and large follow training schedules which would, in the large majority of runners, lead to the shortfalls mentioned above, is perhaps, Lok suggests, due to their very light bodyweight combined with some great genetic advantages in 'reactivity' of stride, shielding them from the detrimental aspects whilst retaining the benefits of the traditional approach.

Lok is candid in pointing out where a suggestion doesn't have any cast-iron science to back it up or otherwise, and that his plans are formed from his learned experience. When criticised on the vast amounts of common ground across his schedules from 1500m to Marathon, he points out that 'traditional' coaching also shares this commonality for much of the seasonal cycle; the reason is that both of the two schools of thought are aware that the 1500m is, simplistically, about 70 to 75% an aerobic event, whereas the marathon is about 99% aerobic; so on that important parameter they are much more similar than they are different (though they are different!).

Lok has coached at a very wide range of levels so he writes as credibly about a 28 minute 10k runner as someone taking 65 minutes for the distance, and acknowledges that, for example, Anaerobic Threshold in a newer or much slower runner is not far from their 5k race pace.

Paid For Coaching

Now let's talk about money and coaching. Forty years ago within athletics in the UK it would have been a very brief conversation. Basically, in the private sector, there wasn't any. There were a very small number of moderately salaried national and area coaches funded by the federation and a few working at the leading handful or so of the athletic universities. But close to zero cases of an athlete paying individually for coaching support.

My perception is that in endurance running there were fewer operating coaches in the club environment though at the modest level I was at it's possible that I wasn't fully clued up on who did what, and where they did it. But certainly, below a very high level, let's say around 30 minutes for men's 10k and extrapolate that level across the distances, and equivalent for women, there would be far less chatter about coaching in general and "my coach " would be a very rarely heard word pairing. If anything, it would have an undercurrent of self importance to it and if the runner was not pretty damned fast could seem almost ridiculous. This sort of environment seemed to prevail through most of the 1990s. Many if not most new breed running clubs had no qualified experienced coach in their ranks and the bigger hitting athletics clubs would have up to a handful of people for all their endurance runners, male and female, aged 11 to veterans and from 800 metres to marathon. It was all done on a voluntary basis and money was just not mentioned beyond clubs reimbursing coaches for some expenses if claimed, though often they weren't. It was and is the coaches' "hobby " (using the widest definition to include any activity that wasn't their job).

Typically and as mentioned above, the leading lights at a new running club might tap into the experienced coaching at an established athletics outfit. So it was with Muswell Hill Runners and Highgate; with Serpentine and Thames Valley Harriers and with Trent Park Trotters and Enfield and Haringey.

Even at the highest coaching level the goodwill aspect was immense. Around 1990 Athletics Weekly in it's In Brief columns (which were over the years a huge source of information and links for those curious to investigate) reported that former national marathon coach Don Shelley was returning to coaching and gave his home address. So I sent him my training framework (intuitively I thought that just arriving at his front door unannounced was probably excessive, so went with the postal option) and other relevant background and goals and we had a couple of helpful exchanges. Clearly from a professional point of view there could be nothing of real gain to him, remotely coaching - he was from Staffordshire - an injury prone guy in London who couldn't even dip under 2.30 in the marathon, but he was apparently happy to help.

If you are yourself immersed in a club currently you may think that the above scenario described above is in fact quite similar to what you encounter in the mid 2020s and in many cases that is true, albeit the in-house coaching availability in nearly all running clubs has been beefed up down the decades. But that is only part of the story and, as the world of running spreads ever wider, an increasingly small part.

The internet changed everything hugely from the late 1990s, relatively slowly at first but then vastly. But before we go there, I'd maintain that even aside from communication channels there has been a big cultural shift within people's perception and expectations of running coaching that reflects both the mushrooming of the services industry in the last 35 years and, a thornier point to consider, the way in which the nation's wealth has become ever more polarised.

People in their 30s, 40s and 50s have grown up in an era when nearly every form of training or tuition or coaching on an individual basis (and, within sports, often on a club basis too) has been paid for. Nobody would imagine that individual coaching in tennis, swimming or gymnastics (to take three of the biggest sports that school age children try) would be offered free. Within the endurance sport niche, it was notable that triathlon, which grew through the 1980s and took off through the 1990s, had very little if any of the historical and cultural amateur baggage of athletics and thus one found triathlon coaching was much more weighted towards a paid-for basis from its earliest days. That its growth coincided with this wider cultural expansion of the services industry was maybe also relevant.

So, as adults over the course of a couple of decades became ever more used to the default that you'd expect to pay for any personal attention from an experienced provider, so there developed a latent market to pay for coaching in running. The internet played a transformative role in releasing this latent demand. Prior to the millennium there were only a tiny number of UK coaches who tapped into this. There was at this stage within the sport still a volunteer default expectation so any coach starting to charge would potentially face a backlash of resentment within the sport. But only within "the sport". That is, the person coaching as a volunteer the hardened 31 minute 10k young guys at Sleekcalf Harriers might also, via the internet, use the same set of skills and experience to coach a forty-something commodities trader in Chelsea or Chesham for a fee. Certainly through the early 2000s the numbers doing this grew. It became clear that once you were in essence a remote coach, 10 miles or 500 miles seemed to make little difference though one needed some geographical awareness and knowledge of the national racing circuit to be credible as the physical distance between coach and runner increased.

The very act of charging for an individual service means that straight away you are "losing" a significant proportion of society purely on grounds of cost and affordability. This would apply whether one is offering people a service in cleaning their house, landscaping their garden or teaching the oboe (Apologies to any volunteer oboe teachers reading this.)

One way or another runners will sometimes talk about paid coaching and make guestimates on how lucrative – or not – it may be. At one end there are those who think there are greedy dodgy dealers 'rinsing' the sport and cashing in any way they can whilst they can; at the other extreme people consider it is a very unstable way to live and can't possibly be a viable way to get a decent income. I think they are both right, depending on which coach is being considered, and can say that neither scenario applies to me. To put a very round figure on it, and ignoring whether there is sufficient demand to make this scenario happen for many or indeed any individuals, if you are very efficient and work a full working week over five days, every week, and you have quick mental arith and can write concisely and quickly and accurately, provide no voluntary time in the sport, and you charge a justifiable but not unduly grasping fee for your work, you could just about gross £100,000 in a year. If you wish to work additional hours, and to stretch the 'rinsing' envelope, and to branch out with non-coaching add-ons like branded kit and seeking followers (and perhaps more relevantly, advertisers) of your presence via Youtube then you could increase this though I have no idea what the numbers may be. None of these additional gigs seem to qualify as 'coaching' though.

Years ago, when Tick Tock had to be spelled like that and meant, only, the sound that clocks make, I used to joke that on a triathlon start line everyone was paying someone else on the start line for coaching, and it was thus a vastly different world from that of distance running. Now it seems that the number of paid coaches seems to be growing exponentially and I suspect that the balance of supply and demand has shifted towards there being an oversupply.

There is also a trend of coaches becoming younger, having fewer years in the sport (let alone as coaches) yet charging ever higher prices for their services. It is one of very few things that in a roundabout way make me glad not to be younger. That is, I'd not want to be setting up now as a coach wishing to make an income, when the market has become so crowded, with so many people presenting such similar profiles that shouting loudest, both literally and metaphorically via social media that I neither use nor properly understand, seems to be the primary way to gain coachees. Clearly one can't fairly lump together these new coaches as one mass, and several are able and articulate and well qualified as athletes and, to a degree, as coaches. Several though seem to have self-assessed to a fast track, based on the amount they charge in context of their credentials.

As to what coaches should really be worth if they choose to charge…. the teaching profession seems maybe the most suitable to compare it to – it has a wide spectrum from Teaching Assistant to Head Teacher and a clear range of levels in between. And, whilst the minutiae may not be transferable, there is some common ground that can inform what a certain level of coaching experience may be worth. Though perhaps this is naïve and idealistic as for some it seems to have become just an unregulated marketplace where you charge as much as you can get away with and/or as much as your own ego suggests rather than what your coaching record suggests may be suitable.

Retention and word of mouth recommendation is by far the main way

I operate and the latter is hugely important and is much appreciated. Google search is also key although I currently wonder if the importance of this channel may be drifting, in conjunction with the growing prominence of the whole social media world.

Even aside from the technology, at which I am poor, the process of regularly showing yourself to the world and, whether subtly or blatantly, selling yourself, seems an odd and ugly way to live. My impression from coachees is that they tend to share this approach to life, which is perhaps why, in an increasingly crowded market, they chose me in the first place. Whether because paid-for running coaching is not regulated beyond the coaches' code of conduct (the breach of which seems embedded within the business model of some coaches) or whether because in the post-truth world you can lie to whatever extent you assess you can get away with, there are numerous pieces of fiction sprinkled around the coaching CVs one encounters.

I am not the most objective judge on this, but from much of what I see, I think that for many runners who are clients of the social media crew, they would race faster, receive better service and pay less if they changed coaches. Periodically I receive new coachees who have moved on and their narrative of why they have made the change confirms my view. All that said, one admires the coaches who stress their "24/7 availability " though I fear the possible consequences of total absence of sleep for the sake of eternal coaching availability.

Various online forums confirm that the Youtubers are not universally liked or respected and indeed some are the subject of ongoing threads of vitriol and contempt. It must be quite a thing, to be publicly chasing a particular goal time in a marathon (nearly always a marathon) and to have so many of your performance peers hoping you fail. It goes against the grain of what is a very generous and supportive community, but perhaps they bring this on themselves.

I find some of the Youtube coaches' content tawdry; video footage of the runner chomping on a peanut butter bagel and glugging down their product-placed electrolyte drink as they execute their pre session fuelling strategy (or "eating breakfast " as some of us old stagers quaintly describe it); then driving to the session venue and doing whatever session is on their tailored agenda.

How this evolving coaching world pans out for me in practice is that, outside the Highgate commitments, about 25 per cent of coachees are women, about 30 per cent are not born in the UK (nearly all from Europe, North America and Australia) and, perhaps reflecting London's professional make up, almost 40 per cent work in financial services. About 15 per cent aren't actually based in the UK although nearly always we have made the initial link whilst they have been in London.

The **www.runcoach1to1.com** website was set up with the excellent technical back up and ongoing online support of Mike Brenard at Webnation who I'd recommend for any small business website set up needs. He offered in particular some sound advice on optimising the search engine prominence of the website which I think continues to work neatly – and, hey, who doesn't occasionally search for their own online presence. When he did a revamp to make the pages more mobile device friendly I asked him if he had any advice on any related promotion I could try as this was well under my radar. I remember that he sighed and said he didn't really have much interest in the "crushing banality " of it all and the two words lodged in my mind as being spot on in how I viewed that part of the then-new communications world.

The very occasional bad coaching links remain in the memory. One young man had negligible running or endurance background and a goal of a sub 3.30 marathon about four months later. I said this seemed very ambitious in the limited timescale, but I would do my best and I was sure he could break 3.30 at some future stage given suitable timescale. About six weeks later he fed back that I was "the most demotivating coach [he'd] ever known" and was ending the link. I was so shocked by this body blow that I didn't ask if he had met other more demotivating people, who happened not to be coaches. He elaborated that he had advised his friends and family not to be coached by me, which seemed bordering on overzealous unless his entire family and social circle were simultaneously on the hunt for a running coach. Curiosity can kill the coaching cat but nevertheless I checked the marathon results in due course and up came his data of 4 hours 11 minutes. C'est la vie.

The coaching approaches online cover a huge range – in the last year these have spanned from a 65 minute half marathoner to a handful who haven't and are not yet doing any running but have been allocated a London Marathon place. Every so often an Enquirer will unwittingly give out info that flags up that I am not the one for them. One little trend is those whose questionnaire responses go into minute detail on nutrition and give the barest skeletal info on their running. This spells out 'Avoid' to me. There have been several in recent years from Goldman Sachs, seen by some as amongst the more voracious of the global investment banks. They've all been very sensible and decent to deal with and my usual take is that they run a severe risk of giving investment bankers a good name. One, when I said that I realised I needed to shape his training to fit in with the high demands of a senior role at GS, pursed his lips and said modestly "senior ish" which I was pleased to hear, the opposite of the supposed self-glorifying stereotype. And who doesn't like to receive a training update sent from that prestigious email address @gs.com?

The three typical questions people outside this odd little coaching world seem to ask are:

• "Do you coach any Olympians?" No

• "How many people do you coach?" Not telling, it is almost never the same number from one month to the next; though it's two digits and isn't 11 or 99.

•"Do you coach any celebrities?" A question unknowingly guaranteed to annoy me.

My very infrequent coaching dealings with people who fall into the celeb category invariably do not last long. The first was perhaps the oddest. The person was in the creative world and pretty much a household name at the time. They communicated through an email address based on their initials. They sent me the standard questionnaire I use for enquirers and in reply to the question "Is it practical to run to work?" they replied no, because their work was done by long haul flights. At some point I linked the initials to a management company name (I guess this may have been set up to pay corporation tax rather than income tax) and was stunned as the penny dropped. We agreed to meet in central London at 5.30pm on a weekday less than a mile from their home. Of all the options to travel, they drove. They arrived over 40 minutes late. This was indicative of how the coaching link played out for the brief period it lasted. In an odd twist, the person did in fact compete in the Olympics, though not in athletics nor for GB and reading the details of how the Olympic selection was secured left a bitter taste in my mouth.

I've had a couple of billionaires contact me through their PA and on these rare occasions I declare my unavailability. In my view the very act of using a PA to seek out and do your bidding to your potential 1to 1 coach is a red flag.

An enquiry came from the CEO of a FTSE 250 company, London's second tier of quoted companies. Aged 50ish, he set out his minimal running routine and level and described how he'd had a bet with a couple of his directors on being able to break 68 minutes in a 10 mile race four months hence. He explained to me the process he would need me to follow. Later that day our emails crossed. Mine was to politely outline why I didn't think the goal was realistic in the context and timeline - "snowball's chance in hell" would have been succinct but not diplomatic. His was a follow up advising that the stakes had been raised and the goal was now 65 minutes. This is not what you go into coaching for.

One of the most memorably positive training progressions was that of a London architect in his late 30s who contacted me one late September to train for the London marathon just under seven months later. He had minimal running background and his aerobic base was built on cycling to work, about twice times 30 to 40 minutes most weekdays. In a 2 kilometre/1.25 miles running time trial at full effort he had been at his limit at seven minutes per mile. With each monthly training block he made outlying rapid progress (without weight loss, so no gains there) and somehow by late April he seemed to be right on the cusp of sub three hour fitness, whereas when we had started the running was so scant I'd not even suggested a goal time as there was no basis for one. He ran 2.59 on the day.

By and large all the longer-term coaching links are with people I like and respect regardless of their running prowess and of course on both sides of the relationship they and I are at some level curating the version of ourself that we present to the other. And it has a defined context.

With the widening spectrum of regular runners, how people view a runner's "commitment " or training volume can sometimes bring to mind a snippet from Woody Allen's mid 1970s classic Annie Hall where he and his partner, played by Diane Keaton, are at their respective therapists. Both are asked how frequently they are intimate. "Oh, almost constantly, must be four times a week" says one; whilst the other replies " Hardly at all, barely four times a week".

In the early Covid months I heard several of the Serpentine guys describe how with all race plans shelved for the foreseeable they weren't really doing any proper training, just ticking along to keep generally fit. This was typically 60 miles a week, with a chunk of it at 6-minute miling just for the buzz.

Coaching Lessons Learned Whilst Running

Having now spent approaching 50 years immersed in the sport, my main adult running days spanned just over a decade from the mid 1980s to the mid 1990s before injury gradually took over. Whilst I did around twenty marathons, with a best of 2.32 and about another ten within three minutes of this rather humdrum level, I didn't particularly see myself as a marathon runner but instead as a distance runner who did marathons. This may sound like a semantic point and somewhat self-absorbed even to make the point, but it's mentioned to illustrate the way the sport is perceived, how it has evolved and at a practical level how runners engage in and train at it.

So as I ploughed on with a typical annual structure of two marathons per year, roughly evenly distributed with spring and autumn races, this meant that for almost exactly half a year I really wasn't a marathoner but a distance runner covering, in the main, races between 5k and half marathon with a smattering of cross country races and road relays and track races. Noone outside the sport would have noticed the difference between someone running say 75 miles per week and not gearing up for a marathon; and that same runner pushing on with 90-mile weeks in the marathon block. Because the non running world only really picked up on marathons and, maybe, because my marathons looked like reasonably solid results versus my 5k and 10k times (but weren't especially, I just didn't mess up at marathons like many did), I was within a modest club level perceived as a decent marathon runner.

Outside the city marathons I had a batch of winner's trophies and Top Three places from the likes of Abingdon, Bungay, Slough and Huntingdon (all sitting prominently on the Waiting List for World Majors status, I assure you), and a couple of 3rd places in the Finchley 20 miler, held on a loop in Hillingdon bizarrely some 15 miles from Finchley. But the marathon never became less than daunting and tricky, basically trying to manage the first two hours such that the last 30-something minutes were just on the right side of excruciating purgatory. If anything, I much preferred 10 miles and half marathons where it felt like racing rather than surviving (54.08 and 71.40 PBs, just to round out the mediocrity in stats). I liked, sort of, being able to rack up 90 mile weeks and I liked, immensely and absolutely, that eating quite a lot of cake could in this light be considered fuelling rather than gluttony; but I never really enjoyed scaling up from manageable 15 or 16 mile longer runs to the 18 to 22 milers that formed the bedrock of marathon prep. They were always hard work, and that extra half hour left a much more grinding muscle soreness in the following couple of days.

What has become clear over the scores of club level coachees I have worked with is that some of them seem more "naturally " suited to marathoning than I ever was even if they are running some minutes slower. That is, once they have found their level at whatever sub 3-hours zone (or indeed for veterans and women it may be over 3 hours to achieve similar performance level based on age and gender) they don't seem to have quite that physical or mental draining effect in doing the marathon specifics. Lucky them. Or maybe in part I coach them better than I trained myself on these nuances.

The point about training hard but explicitly not being in training for a marathon is something which seems in the sport currently to be a kind of dividing line between the solid club runners and the next level down. I'm generalizing here, but there is often a noticeable difference in how the typical 2.40 marathoner goes about their running compared to a 3.15 runner when they are not training over the 3-to-4-month marathon build. The 2.40 person will be running a lot, maybe 75 to 80 per cent of what they do in marathon prep; same frequency; some purposeful structure; a smattering of shorter races. Their 3.15 counterpart may by contrast be rather drifting, lighter running in frequency, volume, structure and motivation; a kind of general fitness for general endurance pattern. I know this from dozens of coaching cases down the years. If I want to really labour the point (I may have already done so) at this level of runner their scope for improvement may in reality lay more in the three months before the three months of marathon training. I'm sure a big part of this syndrome has been the proliferation of generic training plans initially in the running mags and training books, and then of course migrating online, that nearly always span between 12 and 16 weeks pre marathon.

At the extreme, I once saw two fortnightly extracts of Richard Nerurkar's training on a website, taken from different stages of his career (I can't recall where or indeed if he was aware of this use) to make just this point. Both totalled between 105 and 110 miles per week. But look at the details and you could see that the 10k-focused fortnight wouldn't really set you up for the optimal marathon; and conversely the marathon-specific fortnight wasn't really the optimal blend to max out at 10k. The world is somewhat light on books on "How to prepare before you prepare to train for a marathon" and I think it's not only because it's an unwieldy title.

Coaching In Covid

Everyone has their own Covid story and mine was – and I realise I was very much spared the misery, and worse, that the pandemic brought to so many – largely formed by some thoughts I had whilst taking the Spanish sun in the first week of March 2020.

Within the world of club running, it quickly became apparent that with very rare exceptions the runners were too young, too lean and too healthy to be at risk of a Covid fatality. However, as the months wore on the prevalence of Long Covid emerged and it seemed to pay no heed to age, fitness or weight and indeed numerous sufferers from bad long Covid had not been hit with a particularly severe initial bout of the illness. The competitive aspects of running were of course off limits for several months and as the first events cautiously reemerged after lockdowns the particular social distancing requirements meant that some races were restructured to cater for faster club runners only – elite and sub elite, if you will. For many runners (and, no doubt, young athletes across the range of sports) in key developmental years of their youth the Covid phase largely wiped out two seasons which was a massive blow to so many of them – it is in effect an entire age group within the sport.

This trend of some races 'siphoning off' the top levels of distance runners has continued even post Covid and arguably is something that is here to stay – perhaps in part a reaction to the huge popularisation of foundation and recreational running which itself received a boost in Covid.

I had for two years planned to resign from my job and take a chance on a coaching-only self-employed basis. I had even pinned down the resignation date as Easter 2020, to max out the paid Public Holidays over the period. I was fully committed to this plan but then there came that astonishing phase, that lasted about three weeks, where each couple of days the state of the world seemed to change. One particular memory was watching the BBC news on which there were detailed daily reports from Italy and parts of Spain, notably Madrid, that were being particularly severely affected well before the virus really struck in the UK. What struck me was the condolence-like tone adopted by the presenters, creating the tone that the UK was fortunately positioned in some way so as to avoid this plight. Almost as if the Coronavirus had some awareness of and respect for the Brexit thing. The island geography was irrelevant given the scale of international air travel, and it was already obvious that this was accelerating the global spread. One Prime Ministerial utterance that spoke volumes to me, as regards the leader's character, was in his first lockdown speech "We're taking away the ancient, inalienable right of free-born people of the United Kingdom to go the pub," – using a pivotal moment of potential national tragedy to make a performative use of his own purported wit, and using a word that the large majority of the audience would not readily recognise.

So as things moved at pace, I parked the April 2020 resignation plan. In the event, I was furloughed for some 16 months, at full pay (the employer decided not to financially penalise those who were not required to work, who had no choice in the matter) and then took immediate advantage of the redundancy deal that the employer (which had lost millions of pounds of Revenue through having to close its facilities for so long) offered to ensure that post pandemic it cut its staffing suit to fit its income cloth. My age at the time fell just on the sweet side such that the benefits that would normally have been paid at 65 came, unreduced, some eight years earlier.

It wasn't a crushing personal financial blow given the furlough arrangement but in about two weeks through late March over one third of my paying coaching runners signed off as their various goals all went into abeyance, so understandably they lost the motivation to train to a structured programme – plus of course some of them were themselves in difficult and uncertain employment scenarios. Conversely over 2020 there were a few who came to me precisely because their new Work From Home flexibility gave them time to train more effectively and they wished to optimise this, even if for unofficial racing targets. One of the more unusual coaching activities I provided in November 2020 was a Half Marathon time trial for all coachees who wished to partake in Battersea Park, socially distanced as required at the time. In a strange way it was a very enjoyable event, with an inspiring camaraderie brought on by the odd scenario, and particularly pleasing was the one runner who ploughed on alone to complete the full marathon distance, achieving a 2.58 which was his first sub 3 clocking.

A shout out to England Athletics, Endurance Officer Tom Craggs in particular, for piling in with numerous lively and informative endurance coaching webinars over the lockdown – the likes of Aly Dixon, Andy Hobdell, Jess Piasecki and Kiwi legend of yesteryear Rod Dixon (a two-part interview no less) all bringing some zoom-based added value.

8

THE WORLD OF SPORT

Working for it

You might think that with all this knowledge and enthusiasm for the sport, and supposedly educated enough to apply it in some professional way, I should have tried to earn a crust in the management and administration of the sport. I did try very soon after graduating – I went for a very informal chat to the IAAF Headquarters which was then in London's Knightsbridge area, almost right opposite Harrods. I chatted to John Boulter who was then one of the senior management team at the World's Governing Body of the sport. Apart from the fact that there wasn't an actual vacancy and I had not really done anything directly employable in the sport nor really prepared for the interview by considering what I might actually bring to the athletics admin table, there was nothing to lose.

With hindsight it would never have worked out anyway – there's no way a starting salary could have funded Harrods food counter offerings at lunchtime. As I wondered through the IAAF corridor a couple of officers were asked by a colleague what a "lien " was. This is the life, I thought, spending your working day on international athletics with occasional brief forays into the arcane outposts of English vocabulary. Though thinking back, (and one's recall after 37 years can sometimes be sketchy, even on these weighty matters) I have a nagging concern that they may have been dabbling in The Times crossword when they were being paid to fine tune the qualifying score for the heptathlon at the next world championship.

Many years later I had a much closer shave with what have been a lovely job as Major Events co-ordinator for the European Athletics Association; that is, the pan-Europe Federation which sits between National Federations and World Athletics itself. By then I had spent some years in Sport England /UK Sport employment and was also pursuing the coaching side. I remember having a frisson of anticipation when during the interview I was physically handed the folder for the European Cross Country Championships. This was one of my favourite events across the entire sport. The interviewer even used the actual future tense in outlining what I would be involved in, not the conditional. It was a very lively two hours and as my daughter had arrived in the world just three days prior, I was in a somewhat heightened state anyway. I recall that, in an implicit reference to the very humble financial state of the EAA, she joked "The main perk of working for the EAA is that you are working for the EAA". The one specific that was ultimately my downfall was the fluency in a second language requirement. My French limitations have been described above – and not speaking the language for several years had had a predictable effect on my competence in using it - and although my Spanish was coming on gradually it wasn't truly fluent as was required and fell into the third tier of priority tongues after English, and then French or German.

On a purely domestic level I put my name into the hat for a Part Time role with UK Athletics on its elite Disability Programme – basically the athletes who compete in the Paralympics. I had a lively interview with a man who became a colleague as an England Athletics Coach Mentor a few years later (and who had also followed that classic career pathway of English Literature to Athletics Endurance Coaching and Administration). In a slightly off piste lead in to the interview I chatted to one of the small team working on the programme, who was at the time perhaps the UK's leading male Cross Country runner, and he divulged the name of the other interviewee on the short list. Suffice to say that this person is something of a legend in disability athletics and has since gone on to be one of the most recognisable names and characters in disability sports administration. So once again it was all good but not good enough. In sport if you come second you receive a silver medal, in job interviews you get a rejection email and a generic pat on the disappointed back referencing how good the applicant cohort was.

In 1999 Sport England and UK Sport were recruiting people to manage their new Lottery funded programmes which at the time (and largely this is still the case) split quite starkly between World Class Performance and Community Programmes. It's clear on which side of the divide my interests lay so I prepared thoroughly for the interview and made it abundantly clear what I was focused on. My then partner had prodded me to think more widely than my plans to hang around the likes of Bath and Loughborough University or Crystal Palace Athletics Track by reminding me that I might just as easily be asked about what strategy I would use to encourage more Turkish women to go swimming. As it happened, a question almost exactly along these lines came up once I had rambled on keenly about altitude training, sports medicine case conferences, and physiological testing. At that point I took a deep breath, imagined myself working in the Community Engagement Team in the Borough of Lambeth and….. actually I can't remember what came out. But it wasn't very long, or good. I was very flattered to be told that out of the 100+ applicants in that recruitment cycle I was the one who had the fullest grasp of how the World Class Performance Programmes should be implemented and developed so I was delighted to start working on that team in Autumn 1999.

For the Sydney and Athens Olympics in 2000 and 2004 respectively it was hugely exciting to see the full story of how these funding programmes panned out. It was, by some margin, the most enjoyable period of my employed working life and I went to numerous seminars and events and conferences where I would have happily paid to attend the proceedings, whereas it was part of what I was being paid to be at.

Partly it was the content, partly it was the people and partly it was the newness and innovation about the whole set up. As a simplistic overview, my take is that it was and is a very successful long-term investment for buying success at global level in sports that require state-based funding to achieve that level of success. The obvious challenge to justify any use of public money in elite sport is that there are always a host of more obviously essential public services to which it could have been alternatively allocated.

I worked with maybe 20 National Governing Bodies of sport although either by chance or because my objectivity might be clouded, I never had a working link with UK Athletics. I did see all the funding detail sport by sport and it's true to say that the early days showed a somewhat liberal approach to funding of athletics. As an example, there was one year when five GB men, all in the main senior category, in one particular field event, were funded at the elite level. You won't need reminding that the medal hierarchy in Olympic and World Championships has for many decades been that familiar trio from gold to bronze, so the rationale for this generously supported quintet wasn't quite clear. At that initial stage the funding strategy hadn't quite worked out how to support the non-Olympic strands in Olympic sports which nevertheless had World Championship status and elite UK performers. Examples included lightweight rowing, canoe marathon and in athletics the likes of mountain running. So for a year or two there were more top UK mountain runners receiving Lottery support than there were 10,000 metres specialists, as the hilly off-road part of the sport hadn't been dominated by East Africans in the way that long track racing had. Something of an anomaly.

As the national obesity epidemic became more obvious, with its very close links to lack of sport or even basic physical activity apparent, Sport England had to shift its focus more towards foundation or remedial activity, indeed in later years the roles of the 'sports' agencies seemed to sit more closely with public health. The word 'activity' became more dominant as social studies in the sector discovered that the very word 'sport' was itself a big deterrent to millions of inactive citizens. Under pressure from the then-named Department of Culture Media and Sport, the ministry to which Sport England is answerable, the then CEO committed the organisation to deliver a 20% increase in sports participation over 10 years. At a fairly plush organisational dinner held in Loughborough University's private dining area, he stressed how passionate he was to steer this through and that if we didn't share his commitment, we should pack our things away tomorrow. As it happened, his own packing happened very shortly as he himself went off to head a major sports NGB, and for around triple his Sport England salary.

Over the period for which the initial Sport England participation target prevailed the actual growth was barely one quarter of the projected rate. And bear in mind the target was set before London was awarded the hosting of the 2012 Olympics. The participation targets themselves had been drawn from data showing what had been achieved in Canada and Finland in the 1970s. Even the barest smattering of geography and social and economic history might suggest that the UK in the mid-2000s was in a somewhat different state from these spacious sparsely populated nations thirty something years earlier. In similar sporting political vein, when London became the 2012 host city the then Mayor spoke of how this would enable London to become "the most active city in Europe ". Given the data then available for some other cities, he didn't provide a strategy on how to tempt huge numbers of citizens in the likes of Stockholm, Amsterdam, Copenhagen, to get off and remain off their bikes so that London might achieve this delusional aspiration.

The Active People Survey data was for over a decade the definitive tool for measuring physical activity levels in the country. It was impressively granular and covered age groups, gender, local authority (down to postcode), ethnicity and disability. Some of the trends any citizen could easily guess without any grounding in the sector. Some were and are more nuanced. But the one factor that incontrovertibly lay over all the others was that if you were poor, you were much less likely to do regular physical activity than if you were affluent. So there's a case that the industry of interventions, whatever it does achieve, is applying sticking plaster to cover a much deeper wound. As for the 2012 Olympics being a big boost to sports participation far beyond the two weeks of elite sport that Jacque Rogge announced, the rate of adults 'taking part in sport once a week in England' was 36.6% in 2008 and 36.1% in 2016. The Survey was abandoned after 2016 and the 'once a week' indicator was replaced by a 'once per 28 days' criterion. Over the eight years to date of this subsequent survey, the participation rates have, averaged across all age groups, flatlined, though the three categories covering age bands 16 to 44 all show a slight decline. As Olympic legacies go, this has been a real slow burner. Maybe twelve years is too brief a timespan......

Watching Jacque Rogge's Lips

In the mid-afternoon of 6 July, the Sport England Office was in buoyant mood as the famous International Olympic Committee announcement of the 2012 host city approached. At this very late stage, with Singapore hosting the proceedings, Paris was the strong favourite and by all objective criteria was the logical choice. London was seen as a likely plucky loser, but then in the very final stages of the bidding, the combination of the political nous of Messrs Blair, Coe and even Beckham managed to eat into the French majority and the rest is history.

Whatever the many myths and shortcomings of what London 2012 has come to mean, the moment when Jacque Rogge opened the critical envelope was tingling. He formed the crucial word on his lips and read out not the plosive 'P' for Paris but led with the 'L' for London. We went home shortly after, all abuzz.

The next morning, by a combination of Sport England's location, my home address and our childcare arrangements, I came within five minutes of becoming one of the fatal statistics of the 7th July 2005 bombings in and around Kings Cross. My route from North London was the tube into Kings Cross from where I walked south or, if a bus was on hand, leaped on this to travel down Southampton Row. As you may remember, just before nine o clock the bombs were blown up on tubes on the Metropolitan and Piccadilly lines in and under the lines into Kings Cross Station. Then, to show that a twisted mind can really plumb the depths of wickedness when it has the opportunity, as passengers fled the tube station to board buses as an alternative, the suicide bombers (fellow British citizens, though fellow isn't really quite the word) blew up a bus on Southampton Row, just outside the British Medical Association offices. On that particular morning the childcare logistics had worked smoothly and I was carrying out my journey on the ill-fated route around five minutes ahead of when the carnage occurred. It's clearly not an unusual story – the sheer numbers of people moving in and around that section of central London must in practice have meant that at least a few thousand were within a few minutes of being killed in the atrocities. But of course, if you miss it, you miss it, and we were no more damaged than commuters in Sydney or Toronto on that particular morning.

Each sport has its own world and one of the most singular to which I was initiated from Day One was bobsleigh. The physical demands of this are at the opposite end of the fast twitch spectrum from long endurance running, to the extent that some of the world's best came from high profile sprinting backgrounds and particularly those who were 60 metres indoor specialists and in some cases didn't quite match the endurance demands to hang on for the extra four seconds for the full 100 metres. (Different non-aerobic energy systems involved, for any marathoners wondering what can go wrong in four additional seconds of running!). The push start for each bobsleigh run, from a standing start before the crew all leap into the vehicle, is 30 metres, takes just over four seconds and the splits are recorded to the 1000th of a second, so tight are the margins. That tiny extra margin of extra velocity gains a few extra fractions down the rest of the circuit subject to the steering being spot on. So elite bobsleighers were often either ex elite sprinters just past their peak but still keen and able to live as an Olympian; or sprinting colleagues who realised early on that they were just shy of elite level but could make the cut for bobsleigh. The international circuit was almost continuous from early September to late March with a globetrotting sequence of competitions, championships and training camps across the icier areas of Europe and northern America. Mostly in glamorous resorts with high living costs. Almost no normal job could be carried out with this annual 7-month absence (if there is now such a thing as Youtube Bobsleighers as a niche career option, there absolutely wasn't in 1999), so to compete with the world's best a sizeable athlete living budget was essential. In the days of the Cresta Run this kept the sport to the somewhat limited demographic of the very rich inheriting classes but by 1999 it meant Lottery funding was the foundation. The exception to this was the Armed Forces concessions for truly elite sportspeople and thus numerous of the world's best were on Army salaries, doing military duties over the summer months. So, in a strange unintended way the many sprint groups across the UK lay the foundations for the GB Winter Olympic bobsleigh crew.

One notable Sport England colleague with an endurance history was Hamish McInnes. He had been a local teenage running star. Educated at Haberdasher's Askes in Elstree, just a kilometre beyond the Barnet boundary, the school's runners invariably funnelled into Shaftesbury, but he had bucked the trend and ran for Old Gaytonians in Harrow. In the very few races we had both been in as youngsters (he was a year or two ahead of me) he was vastly further forward. He peaked with an exact 4.00 mile as an Under 20, which a fresher at Loughborough, which he never actually surpassed. So on my day one at Sport England where he was Head of World Class operations I was very keen to check that this officer was THE Hamish McInnes. He was an impressive person, very good to work for and his finely honed networking skills were matched by a very quick mind. He has, as of 2024, been CEO of British Shooting for some 13 years and has a 'textbook' career in the upper realms of the UK's sports administrators.

One of the illuminating aspects of the elite Lottery programmes was working regularly with leading independent consultants with high performance expertise. This pool was known as World Class Advisers in line with the programme title though a few shaped their CVs to intimate that they themselves were world class at providing advice. True enough in numerous cases, fair enough. There was a world champion table tennis legend from Sweden; the coach of an Olympic boxing champion who became a great mentor to me; a man who had led the Manchester United physio support when they won the unique treble in the late 1990s; and one of the UK's then fastest ever women marathoners whose speed of thought was even more eye opening than her marathon splits.

One lively feature of the new UK programmes was that a sprinkling of the senior coaching positions went to emigres from the former Soviet satellites. There were Bulgarians, East Germans (most famously Jurgen Groebler the legendary rowing coach) and Romanians. There were numerous Australians plus some Canadians and the occasional Kiwi. The unspoken regarding the ex-Soviet empire people was the doping regimes of their former systems. The UK from the outset had a strong – possibly world leading - anti-doping programme so the assumption seemed to be that by taking on the UK Sport terms and conditions they had to adhere to rigid anti-doping ethics and practices, although it was by pretty clear that their previous nations had state managed doping baked into their system. Indeed reams of documents from the Leipzig HQ of the former East Germany (German Democratic Republic) gave chapter and verse on who did what and when and how much.

Aside from the Olympic sports, we did a review of the Lottery funding channelled to the English Cricket Board as it then was (ECB). It was a one off in the national sports structure in that it was and is the only major commercial sport that has substantial professional revenue based around a county structure. (No doubt the proportion at county level in 2024 has fallen markedly in the last twenty years).

So from a World Class Performance funding perspective, the angle was to examine how best the Lottery funding could tie into the relatively recently established Academies and the county system to ensure the optimal pathway for world success.

We commissioned former England captain Mike Atherton to assist on the insight. Hamish, who would routinely delegate these briefings to less senior colleagues, decided to chair this one with the illustrious consultant. By coincidence my current home is within 100 metres of Mr Atherton (mine is the two up two down former farm labourers cottage, ancient Fiat outside) He is a quiet presence on the village WhatsApp though it's noticeable from his occasional posts that (my wording) even if you have been Captain of England in the Ashes, your Amazon stuff may still just be dumped any place that isn't your address.

Monitoring and Evaluation isn't a trio of words to set the reader's heart racing but when the subject matter is world class athletes and their coaches and performance staff in the heat of Olympic battle the work was lively and thought provoking. Of course, it was public funding and the reports had to follow a generic framework, but the fascination was in the detail. There was one sport where the programme director, targeted medal objective in the bag, had slightly lost professionalism (but gained alcohol) on the final night once the competition was over. Underpants (possibly discarded, reports were ambiguous), hotel corridor chases and fire extinguishers were part of the tale.

Indeed, this was truly the sporting jet set, as evidenced by the briefing meeting I had at Heathrow arrivals lounge with the former Performance Director of Gymnastics Australia as he wandered in "fresh" from having just Qantased across the world from Sydney. Only a pedant will point out that I had journeyed less glamorously across London via the Piccadilly line, swaddled by empty Kestrel beer cans and barely flustered by the 25-minute delay at Ealing South when the train driver succumbed to a non-life-threatening bout of giddiness, triggered when he snuck a peek at the long sequence of digits on his latest overtime payment.

As the UK Sport focus on medals and medals only became ever more finely honed it was perhaps only a matter of time before there was some fallout on the unsought for effects on some Lottery funded athletes. British cycling in particular came under the spotlight both for the doping doubts that emerged but also for some questionable coaching behaviours and the damaging effects on some athletes' mental health. One very insightful comment around these issues came from the former UK Sport CEO who had presided when the programme had been conceived and set up. He stressed in a Radio 4 interview that at its overarching principle (the very raison d'etre) the channelling of public funding was actually not about the elite medal tally itself but more fundamentally about ensuring that young people with exceptional talents were given the optimal opportunity and systems to develop these talents. So the funding was, even before it was about beating the Australian gymnast or the French canoeist, about ensuring that the British gymnast or canoeist could fulfil their talent, regardless of their own financial position, just as the young British dancer or cellist might do, via other funding and scholarship programmes in other fields.

It is a relatively simple task to calculate how much is being invested in elite athletes; you divide the total annual budget by the total number of supported athletes; both numbers are on the UK Sport website. Amongst other things, it shows, maybe slightly surprisingly, that at elite level the supposedly 'expensive' sports actually pan out very similarly to the purportedly 'cheaper' sports. So at the costly end in theory you would put equestrian and sailing and on the other the likes of table tennis or indeed athletics. Once you look at the programme costs it's clear that the single highest cost is for staff, and that regular international travel, sports science and medicine costs don't much alter, across a yearly cycle, whether you end up at the helm of a glitzy catamaran in Biarritz or soaring over a high jump bar in Wandsworth. It's quite likely that a Pole Vaulter carting a handful of poles to South Africa for warm weather training may pay a flight luggage supplement that the distance runner doesn't incur, but that's the nature of the vaulting beast. The very nature of the programmes suggests that if you are going to fund them at all you have to fund them optimally. It's not readily measurable but one can see that if you cut 25 per cent off the programme, wherever you took the 25 per cent from, you might end up losing say 80 per cent of the medals. Given the long-term nature of elite sport (so that puts it at odds with how politicians seem to prefer to operate) it might take at least a full Olympic cycle to manifest itself but that would be the trend.

Steve Cram Off Track

A wonderful runner, suitably chronicled elsewhere, but what about the earthly sporting afterlife?

As Cram revealed in an insightful AW interview, his first commentating utterances left scope for improvement; on Eurosport, he introduced himself and proceeded "Tim Hutchings has just gone to the toilet but he'll back in a minute ". Over the years Cram has to my ears become a masterful commentator. Because I've dipped into so many other TV commentators on the sport, it's clear that to do the role as outstandingly well as he does is extremely difficult. He will be a very hard act to follow and fingers crossed the BBC select his successor using the same criteria which they deployed Cram to this key role. It's rare that one can be such a staggeringly good runner and then perform a totally different job so impressively. (The spirit of world-renowned neurologist Roger Bannister may read this and think, "Yes,indeed.")

On his one excursion at the marathon, he happened to be just behind or slightly ahead of me in the London event. He had given himself the slight disadvantage of running with a mobile wired up so that he could provide a live commentary on his race. He had given himself the much bigger disadvantage of doing very little running training in the preceding weeks and months. I knew this from a reliable source as he was then closely involved, in an honorary capacity, in setting up the English Institute of Sport. This was the Lottery funded Sport England network of venues and people that underpinned the World Class Performance Programme mentioned above. A colleague who worked closely with him would regularly mention to me Cram's weekly mileage in the build-up. It was sometimes in single figures and almost never in the period exceeded what I was doing on my standard weekly long run. On the day, he ran away from me in the last four miles. So the purported marathon specialist couldn't even keep pace with the retired, severely undertrained 800/1500 guy carting along his broadcasting paraphernalia.

I saw Cram in boardroom action as he was on the Funding Panel for the World Class programmes and, in keeping with his character, he was impressively well prepared, highly articulate and on the various matters of discussion would tend to support the case for the "accountable risk" of funding athletes largely in line with the NGBs' reasoned requests. He once came to my verbal rescue when I'd presented the request for English Weightlifting to be funded towards Commonwealth Games medals. With top flight domestic competition rather lacking, the leading lifters were seeking a thorough series of overseas events in suitable tournaments. One of the Panel piped up that the funding request seemed to treat Sport England more as an exotic travel agent, and just before I dived under the table to hide from the embarrassing rejection, Cram thankfully backed up the validity of the sport's argument that if you want to excel at high level international competition you need to get used to high level international competition.

State of the Sport

It was the tour guide in the Baltic who got me thinking. As the coach trip wound its way down through Estonia into Latvia and then Lithuania she peppered her expert commentary with numerous snippets of Baltic culture. She came onto sport and I was pleasantly surprised when she opened with " of course we have track and field at the heart of everything.....". I doubt you'd hear that in the UK even in the unlikely event that a former elite runner is the one explaining how Richard the Third ended up a few metres under a Leicester car park.

None of the Baltic nations exactly dominate the medals table in athletics and with their national populations between 1.3 million and barely 3 million that's never going to happen. But then again, they never appear in the soccer World Cup and don't feature prominently in any of the big world sports. So if they have maybe a dozen of their elite athletes spread across the Olympic or World Athletics championships that itself gives them an inspirational buzz. For these little nations, just being there seems to gain some national prestige. They don't expect to pile up the medals and never have done.

In Britain and the big Anglophone sporting nations (USA, Australia and Canada) things are different. We have history, we have been used to winning lots of sporting stuff and anything less is a disappointment, national failure even. That leaves us all a bit vulnerable at athletics. Compare it to the likes of rugby union or cricket. These sports have very few nations at the global top table and England is never going to be far from the biggest hitters even in relatively weaker eras for the national teams. Athletics by contrast offers scantier prospects for dominance, there are literally dozens of nations with world class athletes, some spread neatly across the events (such as USA, Japan or Australia), some much more limited in range but fantasically good in their strong areas. Ethiopian distance runners and Jamaican and Caribbean sprinters may be the obvious examples.

I'm sure this is, at least in part, why athletics, outside the very brief widows of the Olympics and World Championships, is not very popular in the UK (or indeed the USA or Australia or Canada) amongst the wider public who at best are casual spectators. They don't especially love or even understand the nuances of cricket or rugby or downhill skiing, but they do very primally like to see their nation win. Athletics for most nations most of the time doesn't offer that. The casual citizen isn't likely to think " That's fantastic, one of my countrywomen is the 29th best 800 metres runner out of four billion women on the planet ". (As context, 29th ranked would in theory and 'on paper' leave an elite runner knocked out in the heats of a global 800 metres championship)

It may be largely a coincidence of historical timing but as the global spread of athletics medals has widened, so the sport has struggled in most of its supposed strongholds to maintain profile, financial clout and serious participation beyond juvenile level. One of the Sport England freelance consultants who advised the agency on the media profile sport by sport was a well-known broadsheet journalist who covered most of the sports outside the Big Five (soccer, rugby union, cricket, tennis and Formula One). When the Lottery funding started, he posed the unanswerable question of whether athletics is the smallest of the big sports or the largest of the smaller sports. I'll suggest that if it wasn't in the former category then it would be hard to argue for its promotion around 25 years later.

The Olympics seems to be continually fighting to capture younger viewers for whom the traditional Olympic sports are becoming decreasingly attractive. Every cycle or two a new sport will be introduced – apparently cricket will debut in 2028 in its T20 form. The newer sports are clearly more appealing to older than to younger viewers and participants. With the number of athletes formally capped at 10,500 across the approximately 30 sports in the summer Games this means that if no sport loses its Olympic status to make way for the newcomer, a number of sports have to shed participants which makes qualification standards even tougher. And if a sport is simultaneously expanding its global reach, it can compound the difficult of even qualifying. Depending on how the minutiae of each sport's qualifying structure is set up (for example some sports allow just one individual entrant per nation, however highly ranked a nation's second best may be) one can be in the top 10 in the world and yet not gain entry to the Olympics.

Narrowing in from this wider framework, to look at distance running, it would not come as a surprise if the classic long-distance double of 5000 and 10,000 metres became truncated into, for example, alternating the events at each Olympics. Indeed, the frequency at which athletes double is almost inviting the neutral observer to ask why they need the 12.5 lap race since physiologically it is so very similar to the 25 lapper. And if you watch the finals you'll immediately notice that the leading spots are dominated, if not monopolized, by runners from a tiny part of the earth, a part which is unlikely to be a major revenue stream for the Olympic corporate behemoth.

The UK Athletics medal haul in Budapest in 2023 was a very hefty 10 including outstanding golds for Katrina Johnson Thompson at heptathlon and Josh Kerr at 1500m. Britain also placed highly on the points table for top 8 positions (scoring 8 points for Gold down to one for 8th place), as it always does, and this is usually seen within the sport as a better and more holistic indicator of a nation's depth at world class level. It's a table that is never shown on mainstream media coverage of the sport. The UK nearly always hovers in a range between about 5th and 8th, and nearly always the various relay events help bolster this position. (The USA always heads this table by a large margin; but sadly, not by enough of a margin to give the sport any sort of wide public profile in the nation itself. It's a frequent comment from various medal-toting USA athletes that they are recognised far more readily in the likes of Oslo, Brussels or Berlin than in their native land's big cities.) Paris 2024 was similarly successful for Team GB in athletics – 10 medals and 3rd on the global placing table. The squad secured five medals in relays – the maximum possible, and individual medals in several flat running events, the ones with the highest density of competition. So it's hard to argue that it is not doing very well on that front.

However, on the other hand, across the entire programme of 40-plus track and field events the most common number of UK athletes entered in Budapest and Paris (maximum of three) was zero, with huge voids in the field events. Given that many of the next generation of elite coaches and mentors will come from the current generation of elites, these gaps don't bode well for the next generation.

Even at sub elite level the numbers of adult national/regional level performers outside the flat running events (so, all hurdles, jumps and throws) is tiny, reflecting - amongst other factors, admittedly - the world class funding policy having been in place for half a generation already.

Some decades ago, the basic school age athletics programme was based around the 5-star system designed by larger-than-life Scottish coach Tom McNab, who in more creative quieter moments away from the track was a rare athletics novelist (Flanagan's Run is compelling stuff). He worked as technical expert for legendary movie Chariots of Fire. Over half a century as a coach, perhaps his most illustrious charge was Olympic and World champion in long jump Greg Rutherford whom Tom guided to the fringes of world class.

By the early 21st century Tom was part of the sport's old guard, and I had some lively encounters with him during projects on which he advised Sport England. His novel Rings of Sand, a story in which the Arab petrostates use their new wealth to carve out "ownership" of the Olympics and further debase its values was published in 1985 and was thus prescient given the horde of major sporting events being hoovered up in this tiny area of the world.

The 5-star award gave youngsters a 5-tiered system (with cloth badges, these were coveted for track suit embellishment, at least when on the younger side of adolescence) with scores across five track and field events. You chose your best events but, importantly, had to include one jump and one throw, to ensure a reasonable focus on broader athleticism rather than unduly young specialization. Anyone who just did their best in a few PE sessions would achieve a one star. Five stars was extremely hard to attain; any school year group would do well for one person to earn one of these, two would be rare and nought no disgrace. The large majority would be in the 2 star to 4 star range. Scores were age related through 11 to 18. For whatever reason the scheme was long since abandoned and numerous initiatives have since followed. There are big societal factors at play here but it's arguable that the school year cohorts that were offered the 5-star scheme ended up becoming the senior athletes when the sport in the UK was at its peak. I've no background in education or outside endurance coaching but the 5-star system looks to me a tremendous set up, with the caveat that it needs PE teachers capable of managing the events across the range on offer. Athletics minutiae aside, it surely helps at the margins with numeracy, decision making, and over-arching basic life lessons such as persistence paying off with improvement, and that some people are likely to end up doing much better than others at some aspects of life.

At the other end of the spectrum from those having a go at school, one of the most emphatic demonstrations of the comeuppance for corruption in the global governing body was this announcement, on its own website, in December 2021; "following confirmation from the confederation of African athletics, we note the death of Lamine Diack, president of the IAAF from 1999 to 2015". Twenty-four words, eight of them stating the source, which nevertheless spoke volumes of the saga of greed and corruption that Diack had got away with (a Senegalese citizen, he moved there once his tenure in Monaco ended and thus avoided any extradition). The highlight, so to speak, was accepting bribes of over two million euros from the Russian federation in return for covering up a pile of positive doping tests for Russian big hitters in and around the London 2012 Olympics. I was gobsmacked when I saw this obviously well-considered "obituary" from the organisation. He had previously been described in rather less condemnatory words by his successor, Lord Coe as " always my spiritual president " before the rather gaping gap in his organisation's piggy bank came to light (Coe was a vice president at the time). At times like this one can start to doubt that anything is done cleanly if the temptations to cheat are so easy to succumb to once people are offered the opportunity to do so.

The changes to the sport of athletics and the endurance running sector within it seem to be occurring ever faster (or possibly I'm struggling to keep up or am failing to understand if there is a link across the sports and activities – what used to be routinely described as a 'seamless pathway'). In fact, increasingly I wonder if for most people who take part in 'endurance running' they even see this as falling 'within' athletics. Over the period of writing this book parkrun became embroiled in a heated controversy about how it presents its course 'records. As it decided to operate in an environment that, in my view, sits outside competitive sport I'll choose to look away from it. Though as a means for encouraging people who may have been previously inactive to become more active on a Saturday morning in a supportive environment, it's clearly had huge positive impact.

I find mixed messages. At the very top end of the pyramid, World Athletics has just announced its World Athletics Ultimate Championships, to be held biannually in the years between the existing summer world championships (and thus in Olympic years in the same summer as the

Games). At headline level it looks a good addition because it offers, by the sport's standards, quite large financial rewards to the world's best; around £7 million up for grabs amongst 400 qualified athletes, across three days of events, without an unduly polarised allocation of prize money. It ensures that women discus throwers have the same prize structure as men 100 metre runners, which makes great sense for the sake of the sport's breadth.

My guess is that for the large majority of casual followers and viewers, when this event takes off in 2026, it will be valued and assessed just as if it is a normal world championship. They likely won't notice that the entry size per event will not exceed 16. This may mean that many countries have tiny or indeed no representation at the meeting and indeed many big nations will have no entrants in several of the events if the entry is done purely on performance and merit. If there are medal ceremonies that will serve to convey the effect that it is 'just another' World Championships. That's no bad thing. I wonder though, what additional fan base this may generate beyond the existing one. The events will still be the events, the timetable will be broadly in line with the existing set ups of these meetings and I don't think that the prize money in itself is of interest to casual viewers (who are very likely also to be casual viewers of sports with much vaster cash sums washing round). I'll watch it keenly.

Another more bemusing innovation is the inaugural official European Running Championships to be hosted in Brussels and nearby Leuven in April 2025. The positive is that Belgium has a great history of popular support of endurance running even when its own best are not at the sharpest end. But the details – as they are presented in August 2024 - slightly confuse me. These championships will over one weekend cover 10k, half marathon and marathon. Effectively ruling out any athletes doing any double. Thus the quality of each race is diluted by the timetable itself. The April date is in the heart of the spring Marathon season in Europe so the continent's stars will have to choose between this and the existing races on offer, often in their home nation. Then, the strangest thing, to me. In each race the winning national team will be based on the cumulative times of a country's first twenty-five finishers.

Do the maths. That means that the national teams across this festival of races will need 150 runners to complete their scoring across the women's and men's races. All within the long-distance running sector. I really wonder which federation will "select" such a huge swathe of runners let alone fund their travel, entry fees and, if required, national kit. What sort of level of club runner will be placing as 25th scorer in the supposed National team? Given that the same level of runner will be padding out the half marathon and marathon teams. And of course, how many dozens or even hundreds of other leading aerobic compatriots will be racing somewhere other than Brussels.

I worry that by February I will be hiding behind the sofa to avoid the social media posturings of scores of club midpackers blathering on about "deep in prep for Euros. Can't wait to race for Team GB"

The Andy Warhol quote that "in the future everyone will be world famous for 15 minutes " has been massively overused but since he said this in 1968 it has turned to be increasingly right on the money.

Back at the coal face

"So what work do you do then" asked the BT engineer as he set up the internet connection at my new home, fiddling away with some leads as I tapped away on the laptop.

" I'm a running coach" I said and awaited the usual bemused response. He was keen to discuss his running exploits. These were events where, as I understood it, a large group of runners turn up at a hired location and are chased by various "opponents " in scary costumes in random ways around the location until they've clocked up 5k. Not to be confused with a Southern League 5000 metres, where you will be reminded to line up "feet behind the line". It sounded vaguely like my idea of paintball though I may be off the mark; I've never really been one for things that are described as "fun". (As a child I'd do anything to avoid going to a funfair. Spending two weeks pocket money to "win" a goldfish with a lifespan of about three hours seemed neither fun nor fair.) The engineer seemed a little surprised that I hadn't picked up on this strand of the "sport". He then proffered the supposedly very famous running name of an Ultra/Extreme runner from the USA and when I confirmed my ignorance he clearly thought I was a charlatan in the sport.

This runner has a very impressive and even inspiring CV in life but his highest running attainment in events up to marathon was a Boston Marathon qualifier. Because I hate to lose a discussion on my supposed specialist field I tried, post wiki check, to explain that I had been a quite average marathoner but was plenty faster than this ultra hero.

As he completed his work, I suspected he found the dialogue a little odd. I was left thinking, once again, that the "sport" of endurance running keeps heading off into all manner of weird and unpredictable directions. The easy point to make is that if it gets more people physically active it must be a good thing. No doubt, though in the majority of cases it is in fact just adding another option of activity to already active people. There's the argument that it can offer a pathway to "mainstream " competitive running. Indeed, there will always be someone to provide a case study. And of course, there was the parkrun pathway for plenty. But in my experience the more likely pathway into competitive running is from a competitive other sport, particularly the 'gross motor sports' such as swimming, cycling or rowing.

An early anecdotal but prescient sign of this sea change was in the early 2000s when Athletics Weekly editor Jason Henderson wrote a piece about the magazine's annual stand at the London Marathon Expo. The staff literally couldn't give away the free copies they were trying to hand out to the thousands who traipsed through the rows, many of them seeking out freebies. And this was the London Marathon preview edition, the event colourfully brandished on the front cover. Clearly, they saw the word Athletics and decided that Athletics was for Other People. As the number of London marathon applicants has mushroomed (up to about 800,000 now, a large number of whom aren't even doing any regular running at the time they apply) I stay steadfastly amongst the Other People. There are not a huge number of us, but enough to keep the thing chugging along.

As part of the background for this book I reread 'Running Scared' by Steven Downes and Duncan Mackay (Mainstream 1996) and whilst in many ways the sport has changed since, numerous of the truly big picture challenges (they use the word "problems " which was then accurate) remain and in some cases are actually more acute nearly 30 years on. Fundamentally it seems that the very basic athletics demands of running, throwing and jumping as well as one can have become less alluring. Is that progress?

9

JUST A FAN, THROUGH THICK AND THIN

Finally we come to a hotchpotch of items that aren't essentially rooted in my having been a runner or now being a coach. That is, I just follow the sport – and the endurance events in particular – with a very keen and unshakeable interest (so far, anyway) which doesn't rely on me doing it or coaching it. It is more about curiosity about human endeavour, maximising outlying talent, which can provide exhilarating rewards but also can carry high risks; and – humans being nothing better or worse than human – the occasional outlying bad behaviour.

Athletics on Paper

For many years the gateway to keeping up with the sport was Athletics Weekly. Pre-internet this pocket size publication assumed huge importance for followers of the sport and from late 1977 the annual subscription was a vital birthday present. My very first issue had Kenyan legend Henry Rono on the cover (who died early in 2024 aged 72), and that's maybe fitting as at the time he was taking apart world records at 3000, 5000 and 10,000 metres in a way which gave huge hints of where the global dominance of these events was heading. In some ways just as remarkable as the records were the results he could crank out when well short of peak fitness and there are many photos of him carrying plenty of surplus timber around his stomach and chest whilst clocking 5000 metres times in the 13.20s. Sadly he also set an early example of how alcohol can derail the careers and lives of many a Kenyan talent.

For at least a generation of athletes, coaches and fans the long-term editor Mel Watman's era defined athletics writing and coverage at its finest. Down the years, and in what has become an almost unrecognizably different media world, Jason Henderson did a valiant and equally career-long job in following in his footsteps, with a 20-year spell as AW editor. That his job title is now "Head of Digital" is just one small clue to the changed environment. No single medium can now wrap up the entire sport in its coverage, given all the changes in the last half century, so AW still does its best to embrace a wide range of journalistic strands that fall out from the two words 'athletics' and 'running'.

In my very earliest years of following the sport, the only other UK publication other than Athletics Weekly was RACE, as in Race And Country Enthusiast. One suspects that nowadays this acronym would probably be steered away from, and the word 'enthusiast' is not fully up to modern speed, suggesting an elderly chap poring over his stamp collection or rifling through his array of marching band LPs. That said, it had a well-presented mix of race reports, results and athlete interviews. Its demise unsurprisingly ran in synch with the emergence of "Jogging" magazine.

In a case of financial swings and roundabouts the AW editor Mel Watman, who died in 2021, spent several years supplementing the less than stellar editorial salary with tidy sums from gambling on athletics with a local partner. Given his almost unrivalled knowledge of the sport (and certainly compared to anyone in the bookies' employ) and a smart statistical nous not uncommon amongst aficionados of the sport, he managed to keep a step ahead. Eventually the losses incurred at the corporate end led to them tightening the odds and bolstering their research and thus the incredibly niche career option of gambling on athletics was forever closed off. There are still isolated opportunities for those with a decent balance of sense and money. One such was the 2011 world championships men's 100 metres when Usain Bolt was at the very height of his unmatched career. Before the event, which then had four rounds including the final, started, he was made heavily odds on favourite to win. It was as if nobody in the industry could see how anybody could beat him. But they overlooked that the 100 metres has a false start rule, by which Bolt uncharacteristically was brought down. Well done to anyone who bet on The Field Minus Bolt.

Athletics on TV

For most people for most of my lifetime, watching in the UK this has meant the BBC, and overall I'd say fans have been very well looked after. Perhaps paradoxically it seems that for the purists the coverage is more insightful and nuanced when the event being covered is not a global event, and when there is less chance of a British win. The bigger the stakes for a Brit, the more the coverage tends to veer to the populist.

To take a couple of outlying examples, the coverage of the European Cross Country Championships, held annually on the second Sunday of December, is a real treat. I assume the Beeb realises that only people already entrenched in the sport tune into this 4-hour endurance feast across a Sunday morning, and so the commentary – in recent years nearly always a Cram-Radcliffe double act – is tailored to suit. Whereas, at the peak of Mo Farah's career the screen during the World and Olympic programmes had a clock on the bottom left corner counting down to his race and the tone shifted to acknowledge that the large proportion of the viewers were keen to see a British winner rather than because the intricacies of 25 lap races held huge fascination for them.

Cynical fellow as I can be, I suspect that one reason why in recent years the BBC's free-to-air coverage of the sport has held up so well is because it can be purchased so relatively cheaply, the sport's commercial stock having rather fallen, at least compared to its earlier peak years. I type this in the midst of the 2024 European Championships from Rome, and over the 6 days I'll squeeze in about 30 hours of live coverage – with the BBC providing the European Federation's live stream. At a pinch I'd just about say that this alone is worth the annual licence fee. Which implies that I get to see the Euro Cross for free; and if there's not a single other thing worth watching on the other 358 days of the year – which is a situation that seems to be gradually bearing down on us – then it's a fair deal.

A couple of broadcasting highlights and indeed lowlights occurred around the mid to late 1980s. Addressing the negative side first, for a brief period the BBC lost its UK athletics TV coverage rights to ITV. Simply, it was outbid. Predictably the coverage was horrible for knowledgeable fans, fronted by a previous football commenter wit negligible grouding in track and field and, it seemed, was told to keep it simple and tabloidy. So, many races were presented as simplistic head to heads, which became murky when an athlete other than the two Chosen Ones came out ahead

Much more enticingly, the newly launched Channel 4 televised over numerous Sunday evenings a series of road races sponsored by Gaymer's cider and based around historic city centres. The men raced 5 miles or 10k and the women over 3k (at a time when the longest women's track race at global level was still 3000m and the marathon had just debuted at the 1984 Olympics). Reflecting the times, perhaps 80 per cent of the one-hour programme featured the men's race. The date was perhaps the sweet spot when British long-distance performance was at its best ever strength in depth, money was flowing into the sport and it was still early days in the East African dominance, particularly from Ethiopia. What is striking from the results, which old runners even more nostalgic than I periodically post on Facebook, is not so much that the winning times are eye wateringly fast, although they are indeed very swift, but the remarkable cluster of speedy times being clocked by guys running in 10th to 20th and indeed further down.

About four years later came the compelling but sadly one-off Sun Life Race Across Britain sponsored by the insurance company. Unashamedly using the racing structure of the Tour de France and big cycle tours, over three weeks it covered a big distance, totalling 240 miles of near-daily road races mainly between around 8 to 14 miles. A largely domestic field was spiced up with a posse of overseas elites.

The big difference between running and cycle racing is the damage to the leg muscles, in particular from the impact, and of course the higher the pace the greater the impact and thus the higher the injury risk and the need to recover. There was no modern precedent for such an event so the athletes had to work out on the hoof what sort of daily intensity they could sustain over the duration. Too fast on the opening days and either injury or just under-recovery would finish them off; on the other hand, too conservative an approach would just not do justice to their underlying ability. Perhaps not surprisingly the race structure slightly favoured the marathoners, and it seemed that for those with the staying power a daily racing pace of about 10 seconds per mile in hand versus a truly 100 per cent race effort was viable. The biggest winner both reputationally and one suspects financially was Suffolk star Paul Evans who was at this stage emerging as an Olympic 10,000 metres man and future world class marathoner (his 2.08.52 to win Chicago over 30 years ago still sits high on the UK lists). He has a lively narrative of how, as the daily prizes totted up, in mid race he phoned in his resignation to the shoe factory where he had until then been working. The race wasn't televised on mainstream networks but had good sporting coverage in the media and it's a real shame that a repeat has never been commercially viable. Evans also has a fine line that gives a nod to his initial aborted attempts at the marathon, when he stresses the need to taper substantially in the final week when he suggests the mileage should be" about twenty... including the race."

Athletics Books

It's always struck me that athletics books have always been few in number and sometimes light on quality for what is the Olympics' showpiece sport. Setting aside training guides and manuals, we are left with a few biographies or ghosted autobiographies and not a whole lot else. The biography "entry standard " seems to be a gold medal at global level which narrows the field considerably. And because publishers realise that the world of committed track and field enthusiasts is painfully small, the books tend to be written to appeal to a wider leisure market. I won't name names but I've bought a couple of these and been bored early on. I realise I'm not the sort of person at whom these volumes are targeted

For whatever reason, the USA offers better fare. Perhaps being a niche sport amongst 330 million people gives better commercial options than being niche for a 'mere' 69 million.

But athletics is way behind the likes of boxing and cycling in its literary portfolio. Let's leave football aside, it's a world apart.

There is surely something about location and landscape at play here too. There's only so much rhapsodising to be done over a 400 metres oval track in a modern concrete and steel stadium, or a fast flat metropolitan city marathon route, compared to the thousands of kilometres of dazzling varied scenery that the big cycle tours of France, Italy and Spain cover. In line with this idea, within the niche of running books there is a disproportionately large number dedicated to fell and hill running, which is itself a tiny subsection of the running world. And of the best distance running books, it's notable that the vastness and mythology of the USA landscape tends to have a literary potential that isn't quite matched by the UK hotbeds of Loughborough, Leeds or Twickenham.

Cycling has had its period of reckoning with near universal doping and that itself has produced numerous insightful and highly readable volumes. It's probable that some potentially revelatory running biographies may never be told because the narrators would be obliged to be silent on this. Maybe linked to the culture and indeed huge challenges of pro road cycling there seems arguably to be a greater cast of outrageous, outlandish risk-taking characters. None of the athlete biographies I've read convey characters of this type, which probably helps for these runners' life expectancy if not for unputdownable reading fare. Perhaps another factor is that world class athletes compete, formally, for their national federation, and to varying degrees are funded by it and thus are almost by definition part of the sporting establishment. This may oblige them to be more circumspect in what they can reveal about their sport and its characters. Elite road cyclists by contrast are primarily contracted to their commercial team sponsor (though at Olympic and World championships level they compete on national basis) and so post-retirement they maybe have greater freedom to reveal things.

One of my tongue in cheek favourites was published in 1910, 'Training' by Harry Andrews, and covered the range of athletics events training, and over 110 years later also serves as a great piece of sporting social history. You would be surprised how many times per day the late Edwardian athlete was expected to train; utilising a somewhat polarised approach of long brisk walks and short sprints. You might also be surprised at quite how many raw eggs and glasses of beer and brandy were prescribed to fuel this exacting regime. There's fairly scant longitudinal data of how the pool of athletes fared though one suspects that there might have been an odd mix of hangovers and stress fractures.

Athletics Missed

The closest I came to attending any 2012 Olympic athletics was indeed in the London Olympic stadium in the 2012 season albeit at an event that didn't dominate the sporting headlines, more's the pity. It was in fact at the athletics test event, which was the British universities and colleges sports (BUCS) champs held as ever over the weekend of the Early May Bank Holiday. In what the calendar intimates may be called "early summer " the days were bitingly cold, about 5 Celsius, so it was coat and gloves for the morning sessions. It nevertheless had a unique atmosphere as the students, used to either Chelmsford or Bedford as the usual BUCS hosts, relished the opportunity. It also marked the one and only time my daughter attended a track meeting which she described as "teenagers running around a track". Technically not wrong but not the full story.

As ever the standard was high and as usual there was a sizeable gap between the biggest university hitters of Loughborough, Birmingham, UWIC (in Cardiff) and Leeds, and everybody else. Someone, no doubt a proud former wearer of the famed Loughborough African violet vest, calculated that if Loughborough grads at the Olympics competed as a separate nation, then they'd place somewhere around 10th in the medal table. At the time of writing the Loughborough referendum campaign to seek nation status is somewhat low level so the town remains both geographically and culturally Middle England though there is nothing middling about its dazzling sporting standards.

By May 2012 I'd been allocated my pitiful spread of Olympic tickets; tennis first round plus table tennis. Plus, as a freebie I watched the memorable triathlon races in a packed Hyde Park. It hacked me off mightily that with no hassle and no huge expense, I had been able to pile up tickets for the athletics at the Barcelona Olympics in 1992, the 1993 World Championships in Stuttgart and European championships in Gothenburg, Amsterdam, Barcelona and Munich, nations with which my only links were touristic. Yet in my own country in the sport in which

I'd committed thousands of voluntary coaching hours, I was just one set of rejected credit card data in a highly oversubscribed Lottery. This was the case for the large majority of the athletics "family" in Britain outside the small clan of the official British athletics supporters' club. Come the 2017 London World Championships (currently being trumpeted, with what I believe is not intended as irony, as "transformational" as UK Athletics assesses its bidding plan for the 2029 worlds) I didn't apply though did manage to jump onto the ticketing coattails of a running friend. It was all great stuff – on a par with the other major international competitions mentioned above. Not better, not worse. A few miles west of the stadium there were the trickily rolling marathon races on the last day where the domestic highlight was Callum Hawkins' superb 4th place (which he repeated two years later in Doha). It was notable though not hugely surprising that the crowds on the course were much less thronged than on the annual London marathon race day.

Doping

This is a messy yet inevitable area of the sport and the way it has sporadically cropped up in this book seems to mirror the way it comes up when people I meet in the sport discuss the sport. We never set out specifically to discuss the subject and these aren't people who assume that every elite performance is doped (indeed, sometimes these are people who are doing the performances), nor, conversely, that it is only relevant to the very rare bad apple.

The science of doping and indeed anti-doping is highly technical and not something a non-specialist is likely to master. In addition to the science, the subject becomes inextricably bound up with law, both domestic and international, ethics and sporting politics. It's the mindset of some dopers that intrigues me. Often it falls into an apparently obvious decision taken by an athlete because the financial rewards of cheating versus not cheating tempt them and they assess benefit versus risk. It is probably a very difficult decision for most cheats to make. And so we hear about yet another talented but poor athlete with a limited education and relatively few rewarding other job options receiving a ban. Even if caught and banned, the legal machinations of some besuited people in a lab or office in Geneva or Monaco probably aren't a huge deal to farming communities in the Rift valley or Atlas mountains. The typical ban is four years, with various shorter and longer 'sentences' being used depending on the exact circumstances, so the sport is full of elite athletes who have returned after their ban to have several athletically and financially fruitful years.

The tone of the reporting of doping convictions in the Kenyan press (English editions) is low on moral condemnation. It is surely no coincidence that the doping convictions, across sports, are the lowest amongst athletes born and raised in the nations that, by most benchmarks, are generally rated as the world's most civilised. So, the likes of Scandinavia, Japan, New Zealand, the Netherlands, Germany and indeed the UK. Of course, amongst an entire population with perhaps a few thousand elites across the entire spectrum of professional and Olympic sport, every nation will have its outliers who go against all the ethics that their national cultures aspire to, but some countries make a much better fist of prevention than others. Did someone mention Russia?

I spent years puzzling over surely the most famous ever doping case in endurance sport, that of Lance Armstrong. As he piled on the sequence of crushing Tours de France wins after his triumph over the threat of testicular cancer I was always conflicted by the doping concerns. It was common knowledge that the default amongst so many in the sport was to dope, and of course he was tested prolifically, always clearing them clean. I also saw that in the key time trials on the Tour, the "races of truth" in which each rider sets off solo against the clock for around 50k, over one hour he was typically putting a full minute into the next best. I couldn't fathom how a clean athlete could be almost two per cent better than the best of the rest on the planet. I read what seemed at the time a credible explanation, in the lack of any contrary evidence or any precedent that compared to Armstrong's unique trajectory, that the radical chemotherapy he had endured had altered his physiology such that his utilisation of fatty acids as a fuel source at race pace was somehow enhanced versus all his peers. There seemed a possible logic to the rationale and as a non-scientist I couldn't delve into the chemotherapy minutiae. Also, if he was cheating, I couldn't begin to get my head around his psychology, destroying sporting values simultaneously as he became a major figurehead in raising millions in funding for cancer treatment and research, and achieving a level of national fame in the USA on a huge scale way beyond that of any previous cyclist. But know we all know.

If doping is so prevalent at elite level then it is surely likely that it's not totally unknown at sub elite level though of course one would expect it to be much less frequent. We all make our flawed decisions as we go through life and for a very few it's probable that they err on the wrong side of not cheating in sport. I have felt the urge to delve into truly odd advances in performance on two occasions. One way or another Power of 10, strava and other social media can throw up a wide array of relevant data. Where a good level athlete suddenly pops out a performance (or plural) that seem about 3 to 4 per cent beyond what would otherwise be a super result at that time, it makes me wonder. So for a person established at, say, 70 minutes for a half marathon, in good conditions on a fast course, a low to mid 67 would be quite the breakthrough. If you extrapolate and apply this to a 10.000 metres track race, it's basically lapping your previous best self. That is maybe a more visual impression of the statistic and why a result that as a piece of raw data may not look substantial, can raise eyebrows. In the vast majority of such improvements the progression can be fully explained. In very rare cases the usual factors just don't seem to stack up credibly. Both the two cases in question remain puzzling to me and to numerous others who have similarly delved and pondered and for the same reasons.

Darkest of the dark side

Whilst we have cheating and corruption, the sport is almost never a matter of life and death. Except in one tragically horrible saga in the early 1990s, it was. The coroner's inquest into the death, by suicide, of eminent athletics journalist and endurance coach Cliff Temple puts the events on public record. As Temple was a North London educated boy, a writer (for many years The Sunday Times' athletics correspondent) and a runner who had trained hard to be not very good at long distance running, I had a natural empathy. But even with total objectivity, it was a truly terrible story. The behaviour pattern of Andy Norman, leading athletics official at the time, (indeed, from a British angle, the leading athletics official) always reminds me of Iago, in Shakespeare's tragedy Othello, which is about as low a character reference as one can find. The inquest evidence, and the details of the case described in Running Scared by Steven Downes and Duncan Mackay suggests someone calculating, revelling in his own malignancy, poisoning the vulnerable mind of a virtuous person – shocking stuff in any walk of life, and of course it cut close to anyone involved in athletics. Given the sordid details of the case, which a series of leading athletes and writers revealed under oath at the inquest after Temple had walked to his death under an oncoming train, one particular sentence is still chilling. Norman knew that Temple, who was a father to four young children, was having various personal and financial difficulties and was quoted as saying: "If there is anything I can do to push him over the edge, I will." The Fleet Street obituaries to Norman's relatively early death in 2007 were, to say the least, ambivalent in the context of a man who in many ways facilitated the development of global athletics into a professional sport from its previous era of shamateurism. As one journalist expressed it to me when we were discussing how some ex-athletes seemed to have a worrying blind spot on Norman's well-known ethics, "It's as if getting them a lane in the 1500 metres at Rieti balances out that he was responsible for a man losing his life'

Eventually I had an encounter with the murky side of endurance running, indeed the murky side of human behaviour, that came slighter closer to home. One coach was producing a great squad of Juniors in East Anglia, a relative backwater. We were both appointed in the initial England Athletics team of Area Coach Mentors, to support endurance coaching across the nation. His area in Essex adjoined my North/East London zone. He was the same age as me so had shared the same timeline through the sport. He was technically excellent, highly qualified in the coach education system, articulate, lively and witty, apparently sensitive - when UK coaching guru Wilf Paish died, this coach, who had been mentored by him at Leeds University in his own earlier years, wrote a poignant and thorough obituary in Athletics Weekly. He had also acted as GB Team Manager to various Under 20 and Under 23 squads at European and World Cross country Championships. So, an experienced successful and highly respected man.

These traits were later described by the High Court Judge when he was convicted as a serial rapist, sentenced to 16 years in prison for offences against Under 18-year-old girls he had coached. A particularly repellent aspect of his grooming had included inveigling himself into family dinners with the athletes against whom the offences were committed.

Jon Solly's Too Brief Time Of Glory

Few elite athletes have a smooth senior career and some who manage to achieve tremendous results never fully realise their immense ability, with long term and recurring injury usually the main factor. It's certainly true that in the modern self-dramatizing era one can read that a couple of weeks with a dodgy hamstring becomes 'an injury nightmare' but some athletes really did suffer a raw deal that extended years and years beyond a missed fortnight.

Living in the quiet Chiltern market town of Thame, twelve miles east of Oxford, is 1986 Commonwealth Games 10,000 metres champion Jonathan Solly. I met him, and keenly followed up the contact, when he was taking some initial steps into coaching by contributing to the Oxford University endurance group, and I was catching up with Jake Shelley during his Undergraduate days.

Typical of his modesty, he says that his win was enabled by the East African boycott on account of the UK's ongoing sporting links with South Africa's then apartheid nation. Whilst it's true that this was a factor, the other gold medallists in the men's endurance were Steve Cram (800/1500 metres), Steve Ovett (5000 metres) and Rob de Castella, then the reigning World Marathon Champion from Australia, so it seemed that you still needed to be world class to actually win your event 'minus Kenyans'. In his wake were Steve Jones, then the UK Marathon record holder and at the time the 2nd fastest marathoner in history, and Yorkshire's Steve Binns who the next year would place 5th in the World Championships 10,000 metres. Given that this longest of track events tends to have a long maturation period before peaking, Solly had a startlingly swift transition to the very top. Just 18 months previously he had been no more than a very good student runner, then he shot through the national order, with a major breakthrough at 5000, running 13.30 at the raw age of 20, wining a very strong AAAs national championship on his actual debut at the 10,000 metres event, which served as the Commonwealth Games trial. He recalls "It was only a week before the AAA's that I switched to the 10k. I ran in the Scottish Champs 1500 the weekend before and was thrilled to run 3.43. Alan Storey reckoned that wasn't quick enough to stand a chance over 5k, so why didn't I run the 10? I remember immediately being thrilled at the prospect. 25 laps at Crystal Palace had such glamour. It is the only time in my life that I knew I would win a race. Perhaps athletes only remember things that way when that's how they turn out. Who knows?"

So the Commonwealths was in fact his first race at that level. It was clearly a smart move, given Ovett's change of pace to win the Games 5000.

Solly had had a relatively typical pathway for a talented and bright runner of the time – indeed the outline would still hold true today. He joined Newbury, his local club in Berkshire in his early teens, and – maybe an early hint that the longer distances would be his forte – the small pool of age peers in this mid-pack type of club (in Reading's shadow in the area) meant that much of his weekly club training was with senior teammates, where he would head out on the roads and paths and run close to his limit for up to 10 miles. A relatively raw generic programme nevertheless enabled him to make the English Schools 1500 metres final. He sees this achievement as a moderate baseline, but bear in mind this is around 1980/81, with UK men's 1500 metre runners the envy of the world, and he has joined the fastest 12 of his age group from the whole country. To show how student sport at the time lacked the communications we now take for granted, when he joined Durham University as a fresher, he was initially entered in their C team for some cross country relays as no one had picked up on his schoolboy results.

In a classic case of making your own luck, Solly was in Durham at the stage when UK coaching guru Alan Storey was developing his own coaching in the city where he worked (for Nat West Bank). A bookish and highly reflective type, at one of the UK's most prestigious universities, Solly was never particularly drawn to the graduate 'milk round' for a supposedly traditional graduate career, and the very small number of distance runners who can put 'professional runner' as their job didn't have a university career pathway beyond just running very fast and finding a manager with scruples and an extensive address book. So, his running prowess did for a brief starry period create what many runners would consider a dream lifestyle of lots of training at times that suited him, international racing and travel experiences, ongoing improvement, some level of recognition, and a handy income, all at age 23. This helped the transition from student to athlete, at a stage when he declared in an interview 'I had to decide if I wanted to be an alcoholic or an athlete' – he was known for being a very enthusiastic partaker at the main university post-race socials. In one of those 'harsh but true' statements that serious runners have to grapple with, he was advised by his coach that a bit of carefully monitored weight loss would assist his performance – at just shy of 6 feet/1m 83, he was under 11 stone (70 kgs) at the time – and so reduced to a racing weight of just over 10 stone (64kgs). He describes with glee how in a less pressured midlife 'I have now started eating butter again after 25 years. I love it'.

But things weren't so rosy for long. Various injuries, nearly all lower leg related, continued to sideline him so he went from peaks to troughs with a worrying frequency. On the track, he never rekindled the golden few weeks he had in the early summer of 1986, at an age and developmental stage when he should have still had plenty of scope to improve. Perhaps not surprisingly, given what was clear of where his talent seemed best suited in the track endurance spectrum, a move to the marathon beckoned and he had some decent results, with three or four results in or around 2.12. Indeed he debuted with a 2.12, just missing the race win in Twin Cities, Minnesota, and recalled that Storey's objective appraisal post-race was 'At least that shows you won't be crap at the marathon'. He reflects "To my immense frustration I ran 2.12 and bits three times. I even think two of them were the same time. 2.12.07."

These helped keep the wolf from the door (he was living in Seattle at the time and working part time in a running shop) but his track prowess and glimpses of longer distance ability (including a fantastically quick road 15k, still one of the fastest ever by a GB athlete) all suggested that given a sustained period of injury free training, plenty quicker was under the bonnet. Gradually the gaps between injuries became briefer and the viability of actually living as a pro runner became ever more challenged. Those close to the sport would read in Athletics Weekly of him winning tough regional league cross country races with almost no training background, and then the next niggle would set him back once again. He describes how the final tough decision that 'enough is enough' came in his mid-30s, when his sister pointed out how painful it was to see, how destructive it must be to him, to keep building his life and hopes around something that was just not going to happen.

At a coaching seminar in London, Solly describes how any runner is trying to find race days when everything that has been worked for clicks into place and the result is just what one had hoped for; and that he had just two occasions of this experience.

Talking to Jonathan about the state of the sport, it's surprising how far he has drifted from involvement with it. Part of his detachment results from how jaundiced he became at what were obvious (to him at the time and to the author and others with hindsight) performances achieved by doped athletes, with EPO being the most likely drug of choice. "I'm bemused by what has happened to athletics and often wonder what my teenage self would have thought if he'd been told how, in my 60's, I would have totally disengaged from a sport I once worshipped". It was 2001 before EPO tests were designed that became legally valid so at this early stage (the drug started being known to be used for endurance sports in about 1985) it was undetectable.

He now lives a happy busy life with his wife and two daughters. The shelves are lined with reams of vinyl LPs and books and there's no sign of a trophy or medal cabinet. In his typical self-deprecating maverick way he describes how his overall pathway through life has conspired to make him 'unemployable' and he is probably the only person whose CV shows bespoke furniture maker ("I make things I can't even begin to afford" he reflects), Commonwealth Games Gold Medallist and

Durham University (Economics and Politics).

Steve Jones - barrier breaking by instinct

Early October 1984. I had just arrived at the scraggy terraced house near to Iffley Road track and had unpacked the bags for the autumn term just about to start. I set up the portable TV and turned on the Sunday evening news just as it headed into the sports section. Stunningly, the lead item was footage from the Chicago marathon and the news that Welsh runner Steve Jones had just broken the world record, running 2.08.05 in his first completed marathon. Pre internet days the previews of big events were far fewer and less accessible so very few outside the inner circle would have been aware that this was on the cards. It was quite the breakthrough by Jones who was and remained an outstanding 5k and 10k and cross country runner and on paper would have been likely to do well at marathon, but this was something else. His UK record (later improved to a mighty 2.07.13, then just one second shy of the world record which had moved on from his own Chicago mark) stood for some 30 years until Mo Farah took 90 seconds from it. Two others (just two, and nearly 40 years on) have very recently edged faster though all the data about the new shoes' performance gains surely confirm that Jones ran intrinsically better times.

Because there has been no biography of Jones' life and racing career and perhaps because he is not a publicity seeker, indeed quite the opposite, the amount of information circulating about this ground breaker is rather scant and more than one version is trotted out. He was by his own account a regular smoker and drinker through his early to mid-teens whilst casual football was his only ongoing sporting outlet. When he turned to running, he made truly rapid progress and the journey from cigarettes to running for Wales was dazzlingly quick.

He was in the RAF as a corporal for the period of his running career before turning fully pro in his later years of peak performance, and it's not clear how much of a year-round full time working commitment was required. Essentially, his terms of employment are no one else's business but anyone with an interest in the details of outstanding performance will seek to gain a holistic picture of the set up surrounding the performance. At the time the RAF (and Jones' long term coach Alan Warner was also in the same service) could have notionally competed with reasonable success as an independent nation at men's long distance given the incredible talent it had in its ranks, far more than among the navy or army ranks.

In another coincidental piece of recent reading, whilst drafting this I was poring over the excellent Running Hard by Steve Chilton (Sandstone Press 2017) which majors on the fell running rivalry in the 1980s between Kenny Stuart and John Wild. The latter happened to be an exact contemporary colleague of Jones in the RAF (indeed a training partner whilst both were stationed at RAF St Athan in south Wales) and whilst, unsurprisingly, we don't get Jones' work rosters laid out, it's clear that whilst the Forces leading athletes were well supported in their sporting careers they also had to put in plenty of hours in the day job.

A running magazine published a 6 week of training he did prior to one of his fastest marathons and, as it involved a race or two and some international travel, it happened to average "only" about 85 miles per week. In the ongoing absence of anything else of comparable detail, the myth that this monumental marathon level was achieved off a rather light volume was circulated. And recirculated. There is, though, a chain of website chat which backs up that 100 miles was more typical of peak Jones which seems a more likely volume, rising a little more in the core of marathon prep. Indeed numerous anecdotes from old interviews from Jones himself confirm this. He almost never trained with a stopwatch and even by the standards of the 1980s he trained highly instinctively and by perceived effort. (The exception would have been track sessions using the standard 400 metres lap). Thousands of current runners have far more precisely calibrated training plans and logs. So even today we can't get a detailed handle on how he split his training into different paces. We can only assume that for example his 16 x 1 minute reps were at faster pace than his 4 x 5 minutes reps. There was remarkably little easy/recovery running and even among his peers of the time he had a reputation for pushing the envelope in much of his steady state running. Indeed, possibly some common ground with the earlier Double

Threshold Before It Was A Thing style of Ron Clarke described earlier.

One article stated that in a "typical " week he would race on both a Wednesday for the RAF and a Saturday for his club Newport Harriers. Really? One Saturday when I can testify he raced in the RAF vest was 13 days after his Chicago triumph when he pitched up at Shotover Park to the east of Oxford to race against the University on a really gruelling cross country course. It was strange going to the start line with the newly established legend just a few metres along the muddy field. Though within a minute or so of the start gun the gap was a much larger number of metres. His 2.07 run was even more remarkable, not just by virtue of being 55 seconds faster. But because he split the first half in a stunning 61.52, less than two minutes shy of his best (itself a Half Marathon time that lasted decades as a UK record) and then held on. None of the world's leading times are now ever run in this fashion.

From what I've read down the years I've thought if Jones extraordinary physiology and mindset had been slightly differently channelled, he could have set a marathon time for the ages, a good two minutes quicker than he achieved. All totally hypothetical of course but globally recognised marathon guru Renato Canova has gone on record more than once with just this view.

Almost thirty years after his heyday Bud Baldaro arranged for Jones to do an interview with him at a UK Marathon Seminar, with the legend flying over from his long-term Colorado base for the event. He came across as a quiet easy-going humble character, with no ego, no regrets and offering no 'secrets' to his success. Like any runner, the only running career he really knew was his own so that was his 'normal'.

Coe As Politician

Having briefly mentioned earlier a snippet of Seb Coe's club running activity, this can be set alongside a political snippet indicating how the nature of the role obliges practitioners to swim with the tides. Thus, in early summer 2020 with the world in lockdown, to its credit the World Athletics federation pieced together a series of individual pole vaulters vaulting in their own back gardens, competing remotely against each other. Better than nothing, and it kept international athletics on the map, but it clearly falls some way short of a Diamond League meeting, let alone the Tokyo Olympics which were of course intended to be the highlight of 2020's summer. Coe expressed how delighted he was to "see the return of live athletics". Several months later and, again to give major credit where due, WA did indeed set up some actual Diamond League meets that met the requirements of social distancing and covid testing then in place (no spectators, a constraint which continued through to the rescheduled Tokyo Olympics in August 2021). At this stage Coe declared words to the effect that we'd had our fill of pole vaulting in athletes' back gardens.

He has had an extraordinary life. Perhaps his very name obliged him to be nimble both in body and mind. As legendary coach the late George Gandy put it, recalling his days of coaching Seb Coe at Loughborough, in his Geordie accent "Where I went to school, if you were called Sebastian you had to be able to run fast"

Dave Bedford Down The Ages

It seems fitting to close the full lap that comprises this book with a brief profile of someone who fully fifty years ago used to canter past my front door whilst training in North West London, to fulfil his own potential over 25 laps, and who unknowingly sowed the seed that brought me into and kept me in the sport.

I meet Dave in Hendon and given that he has been heavily involved at the very sharpest end of the sport for over 55 years it's not obvious where to start and what to focus on. What is clear is that the brash reputation is very much not the full picture as he is in reflective mode as he considers the lengthy sequence of experiences he's had.

The well-known headlines are that he progressed quickly at longer endurance in his mid to late teens, trained vast mileage (his mid lecture naps at teacher training college were the result of running three times daily rather than lack of curiosity in the content), capped it with a 10,000 metres worked record in 1973, was outrun by runners with much sharper changes of pace in the big international championships and his peak years were severely punctuated with injuries and the elite career was largely over by age 26. So, simply, what made him excel also broke him, shortchanged him at the closing stages of the biggest races and made him an ex-athlete at an early stage. Like numerous classic early 1970s rock stars but with huge mileage his version of other "doses" and thankfully a much longer and more fulfilling life. He was not initially a standout when he started training; early results in under 15s included 2nd in Hendon schools, 7th in Middlesex schools and 73rd in English schools. Bear in mind that the latter, certainly in the mid-1960s, was a fiercely strong race so the gap between say 10th and 70th was fairly tight though one position looks vastly superior.

He says that once you choose a running coach "your [running] life is set" and he stresses that as a senior (from age 20) when the monster miles were racked up it was Dave who proposed the approach, not a coach-imposed demand.

Talking to Dave about his 'defeats' he has no regrets and to his credit makes no mention of the ethics of anyone who beat him. I'll point out though that his peak years fell in the brief window when blood doping (which substantially raises oxygen carrying capacity and thus makes the runner's aerobic ability higher almost overnight with the extra blood infusion) was practicable but not yet either banned or detectible. Lasse Viren, legendary winner of four Olympic golds in 1972 and 1976, has a carefully worded statement on the matter ' We did nothing that was illegal at the time' which I think tells you what was going on. Dave says of his own disappointment in Munich 1972 "The occasion got to me". The last lap of the European Championships 10,000m race from 1971, another race in which he toed the line with high hopes, is on Youtube. It's a quite staggering piece of end-of-race speed by the three medallists, (almost exactly the same splits as Mo Farah was doing over 40 years later) and even 50 years on is visually stunning. I'd say it seems incredible in the literal sense of not being credible within accepted training and performance ethics.

In the pre-professional athlete era, as soon as he started his role with the International Athletes Club he spoke to every soccer club (92!) in the old Football league and negotiated free physio treatment for British international reps. He mentions former senior federation manager Arthur Gold and IAC secretary Derek Johnson (1956 Olympic silver medallist at 800 metres) as early important mentors and says the latter "saw something in me". I ask what he thinks that "something " was and he suggests integrity, the capacity to present a clear case in a discussion, and the ability to listen. So it seems that in light of all his subsequent roles he became a skilful negotiator. After the IAC role and a not dissimilar role in the Southern Counties' association, where he worked on keeping the area federation in touch with the new breed road running clubs who increasingly were providing its membership income on top of what came from athletics clubs, he moved to the London Marathon in primarily a marketing role. He stayed there for the entire rest of his employment career, over 30 years, with close to 20 years as Race Director.

This role worked with the official CEO Nick Bitel who had a legal background and with, at various stages, Alan Storey as Technical Lead and Tim Hutchings as Elite Athlete Director. This 30-year period spanned the second huge growth spurt in road running where arguably for the majority it evolved from "sport " to lifestyle. I remember at an endurance gathering in around 2010 Dave said that nowadays if someone asks you "Who are you running the London marathon for?" the expected answer is not Cardiff AC or Herne Hill Harriers but the name of "your" charity.

I'm curious as to how he sees the sport in 2024. He says that at all sub elite levels it is "under real pressure" from the increasing lack of volunteers and officials, and that the public interest in the elite end has had a major decline in "credibility " because of the assumption of doping. This leads to declining media exposure and so the cycle is hard to break. He believes that governing bodies have been slow to acknowledge this and not as effective as they might be in addressing it. Like many sports it has been "crowded out" by football. He compares the situation to the owner of a house whose structure is rotting with woodworm dealing with its potential sale "by painting the walls and tidying the garden ".

He references a recent FA Cup quarter final between Liverpool and Manchester United, a seven goal thriller which he had found compelling (he is a Spurs supporter so his judgement isn't always spot on) and flagged up that it mattered who won; which is what differentiates it from so much top level athletics, where the Diamond League "circuit " is presented as, amongst other things, a way to accumulate qualifying points for the Diamond League "final ". The only significant performance difference in the final compared to the previous meets is that the prize money is somewhat enhanced, so that, say, $10,000 from an earlier meet might be enhanced to $25,000 in the final. Hardly a structure to fascinate casual followers.

In some illustrative nostalgia Dave recalls how in the late 1960s ahead of the inter counties cross country The Daily Telegraph, always the broadsheet which gave the sport the widest coverage, ran several days of preview articles in which it ran through the prospects of the leading county teams. So clearly the sport at the sharp domestic end had high public interest. Imagine a modern-day Telegraph with the teaser "tomorrow; insight into Kent's cross-country squad". Another world.

The weekend after we met, the World Cross Country Championships in Belgrade , which brings together many of the fastest 5k to half marathon runners on earth, came and went with zero coverage by the UK's leading newspapers. To its credit the BBC online provided full live coverage with the expert commentary of Tim Hutchings and Paula Radcliffe, both multi medallists in this very event. One assumes that the marginal cost to the BBC for such events is now modest. Whilst it continues, it is a godsend for the cognoscenti who can luxuriate in the ad free impartial coverage. Though it's fair to say the nation's sports bars were not thrumming with debate about Abbie Donnelly's excellent 20th place in the women's 10k or young Will Barnicoat also performing outstandingly in 27th. Hutchings talked about the " huge" prize money which was headed by the senior individual medallists grossing $30,000, $20,000, $10,000 respectively in a meeting which has no appearance fees for these global elites.

Dave believes the world federation has missed a big trick in the battel to reduce doping by not using a legally valid clause by which pro athletes with a doping ban could only return to competition after their ban once they had repaid all sums known to have been earned whilst assisted by Performance Enhancing Drugs. He believes that this big financial disincentive would vastly reduce the numbers doping, which at elite level he estimates at around 30%. I am slightly surprised at this high figure and Dave chooses not to comment on whether this rate varies plus or minus with different nationalities (though official lists of sanctioned athletes give some clues on this).

He thinks that Federations at global and UK level have lost sight of the burning ambition of elite athletes to compete at the Olympics, even as their earning capacity in the sport is also a key factor that pushes and motivates and indeed retains them. He suggests that the ever-tightening global qualifying standards (which means fewer athletes and thus less actual live athletics per session, a direction largely led by TV expectations) layered on top of UK selection criteria that confines the team to "medal/ top 8 potential " further cuts into the numbers of elite athletes who stick at the sport. He firmly believes that if athletes qualify but are not deemed worthy of federation Lottery funding or selection, they should still be able to compete on a "self-funded" basis and is convinced that within their own networks and community they would all be able to support their participation on a quality assured basis to match that offered to fully funded athletes. (My view had been that the self-funded option in theory could leave athletes vulnerable to sub optimal final prep. For example, long haul flights with stopovers to cut costs; excessive jet lag; noisy over-heated accommodation situated far from the athletes' hub; lack of a federation "voice " for any matters that may arise over transport or accommodation or health outside the field of competition itself).

Interestingly he dismisses as "bollocks" the standard argument that selecting supposedly lesser athletes who are knocked out in their heats gives a negative vibe across the closely knit team which can just take that marginal winning mental edge off a potential medallist. I've never been in any sort of position to assess this with any credibility; only those who have been there can assess its validity.

I ask him if my suggestion of who has been by far the most (arguably, the only) pioneering UK long endurance coach in the last 40 years correlates with his observations and am reassured that I'm on the same page. Dave himself has very minimal advisory links with any athletes. He's never had the time to coach (he mentioned that his career-long coach Bob Parker typically saw him four times per week, and Dave was just one of an illustrious squad, men and women, that Parker coached) and estimates that around twelve runners have sought his advice down the decades.

I ask Dave to pick out the biggest thrills he's had in the sport, excluding his own achievements. So from his almost 60 years immersed in the cut and thrust he picks out the London marathon 2002 when Khalid Khannouchi set a world's best of 2.05.38 to beat Paul Tergat and Haile Gebreselassie who were both then at their awesome track and road racing peak and Paula Radcliffe won in her debut marathon in 2.18.56, then the world's second fastest ever time; Bob Beamon's other worldly long jump of 8 metres 90 centimetres in Mexico 1968 (56 years on and just two longer jumps have ever been achieved, by 1 and 5 centimetres, and Beamonesque is, just about, an adjective in its own right outside the niche of long jump); and the achievement of Michael Watson overcoming horrific near-fatal injuries incurred in a brutal boxing match. He completed the London marathon in 2003, spreading his effort over 6 days of struggle. So sometimes the very act of participation is itself the huge accomplishment. The book started by mentioning the multitude of runners' tales, and so can close by briefly referencing a vastly different one from mine.

AFTERWORD

It's early August and a few waking hours capture in microcosm the huge range of people and events that now fall within our sport's compass.

It's another Paris Olympics athletics evening and even with very little distance running in this session there is literally a thrill a minute as the BBC is in top presentational form. The men's javelin is won by a thrower from Pakistan, population 235 million, taking only its second ever gold medal across all Olympic sports. Bronze goes to Grenada, population 125,000. Meanwhile against the might of the USA the Men's 200 metres is won by a Botswanan, population 2.3 million, the winner running in tribute to his mother who died just two months earlier. We are treated to a stunning world record in the women's 400 metres hurdles with such a jaw dropping time that it would almost have made the final in the 400 metres flat. None of these events are in "my" distance sector yet I find it compelling and can't really understand how anyone wouldn't. At a sports-politics stretch, I note that Team USA is collectively piling up the athletics medals at a quite staggering rate, even as the nation seems to be pulling itself apart in every way short of civil war.

I have a coaching zoom with George in Cyprus, and we discuss, not entirely in jest, whether endurance athletes on the verge of elimination in these tight Olympic heats, might "facilitate " a fall to then be advanced to the next round, so frequently does this scenario now occur.

Meanwhile I have a WhatsApp from an enquirer who asks my

191

availability for early morning one to one coaching sessions, even though I've sent them my website info that spells out that this is not an option.

Highgate whippet Jacob Allen calls and we discuss training bumph and then get steered onto the thorny subject of the huge sporting advantages of private schools in UK versus the state sector. Jacob had moved from a previous post at prestigious Dulwich College to the grittier inner-city school where he now finds his role more fulfilling. We chat in the context of Team GB at the Paris Games being 33% privately educated, almost five times its proportionate level.

To round off the One Day Snapshot there's a lively email from a coachee who is aspiring to break three hours in the marathon. He discloses that his partner is due to have their first baby in six months and as life changes, he expresses some mild concern that age may be against him. As he is 33 years old, and in two days the Olympic Marathon startlist is spearheaded by the dual endurance legends of Eliud Kipchoge, 39, and Kenenisa Bekele, 42, I'm pleased to suggest that age is on his side.

August 2024

ACKNOWLEDGEMENTS

Many thanks to Paula Waldron for her editorial input. And to Rob Wilson for acting as reader for various sections and taking on the marketing role for this book.

Particular thanks for the cover design and typesetting to David Wardle(boldandnoble.com). David was a 29 minute 10k and 65 minute half marathoner at his peak and provides a great dynastic link in books about running, in that his father Wilf was also a designer and top runner whose work enriches the exemplary Brendan Foster biography by Cliff Temple in 1978, one of the earliest and best books I read on the sport.

Also to all the various athletes and coaches and key others who I worked with to provide the profiles within: Jacob Allen; Stella Bandu; Dave Bedford; Izzy Clarke; Will Green; Alex Lepretre; George Loucaides; Dave Newport; Martin O'Connell; Ben Pochee; Jake Shelley; Paul Simons; Gavin Smith; Jon Solly; Dave Sweeney; David Turner; Chris Wright. Thank you for your time and for checking and consenting to what is presented. And to Mara Yamauchi and Chris Jones for reading the contents to inform their supportive comments.